Osprey Modelling • 39

Modelling the F4F Wildcat

Mark Glidden

Consultant editor Robert Oehler • *Series editors* Marcus Cowper and Nikolai Bogdanovic

First published in Great Britain in 2007 by Osprey Publishing,
Midland House, West Way, Botley, Oxford OX2 0PH, UK
443 Park Avenue South, New York, NY 10016, USA
E-mail: info@ospreypublishing.com

ISBN 978 1 84603 110 6

Editorial by Ilios Publishing, Oxford, UK (www.iliospublishing.com)
Page layout by Servis Filmsetting Ltd, Manchester, UK
Typeset in Monotype Gill Sans and ITC Stone Serif
Index by Alison Worthington
Originated by United Graphics Pte Ltd, Singapore
Printed and bound in China through Bookbuilders

07 08 09 10 11   9 8 7 6 5 4 3 2 1

A CIP catalogue record for this book is available from the British Library.

FOR A CATALOGUE OF ALL BOOKS PUBLISHED BY OSPREY MILITARY AND
AVIATION PLEASE CONTACT:

NORTH AMERICA
Osprey Direct, C/O Random House Distribution Center, 400 Hahn Road,
Westminster, MD 21157, USA
E-mail: info@ospreydirect.com

ALL OTHER REGIONS
Osprey Direct UK, P.O. Box 140 Wellingborough, Northants, NN8 2FA, UK
E-mail: info@ospreydirect.co.uk

Photographic credits

All photographs appearing in this book were taken by the author.

Acknowledgements

I am indebted to the following people and am grateful for their
assistance with the preparation of this book:
Marcus Cowper, my editor, for his help and guidance during this
project. Stan Spooner, who, having experienced the joys of being
an author himself, answered my many questions. Karl Madcharo,
the keeper of all modeling knowledge. Fred Medel of Tamiya,
America, for donating the Wildcat kits used in this book. Mike
Budzeika, for his assistance with the proofreading of the text and
his eye for critiquing models. Sharon Maguire and the staff at the
Palm Springs Air Museum for allowing me to photograph their
FM-2 Wildcat. Al Valdes and the staff at the San Diego Air &
Space Museum for allowing me to photograph their F4F-4
Wildcat. My wife, Sherry. Without her encouragement and
support (not to mention patience), this hobby never would have
become what it has for me and this book never would have
been completed. Thank you Sherry, for everything.

Dedication

This book is dedicated to my wonderful son Sean, who while not
a modeler himself, always found time to stop by my worktable
with complimentary words and encouragement.

Contents

Introduction

When I got back into modeling about six years ago after a 25-year hiatus, I discovered to my dismay that the hobby had changed a great deal in my absence and I had a great deal of catching up to do. I started reading everything about modeling I could get my hands on, whether it was magazines, books or the internet. So anxious was I to get back into the hobby I purchased the Tamiya Fw 190D-9, naively buying every piece of resin and photo-etch I could get my hands on for the kit. Never having used either medium before I was, to say the least, in a little over my head at the time. But what a learning experience it was. And it was fun.

Learning something new, getting some new ideas and improving one's modeling skills is what this book is all about. At the end of the day, if I have been successful in encouraging a modeler to try something new or help him achieve a new level in his modeling, then the making of this book will have been worthwhile.

While I learned more about the Grumman Wildcat than I ever wanted to during the preparation of this book, I am not by any means an expert on the subject. To those more enlightened than I, I apologize in advance for any inaccuracies.

A brief history of the Grumman Wildcat

The Wildcat is one of those historically significant aircraft that almost never came to be. In fact, it was through the misfortune of others that it became the Navy's frontline fighter for the first year and a half of World War II.

The Wildcat's development paralleled that of the Brewster Buffalo, and it was the Buffalo that the Navy chose over the Wildcat as its first operational monoplane fighter in 1938. However, hedging its bets, the Navy continued development of the Wildcat. When the Buffalo proved itself not up to the task in the hands of Allied pilots in the Pacific, the Navy turned to the Wildcat.

The F4F-3 was the first version of the Wildcat to enter service with the US Navy in December 1940. The -3 was noteworthy in having only four wing

The granddaddy of them all – the Monogram Wildcat kit. Kind of makes you wish for the simple days, doesn't it?

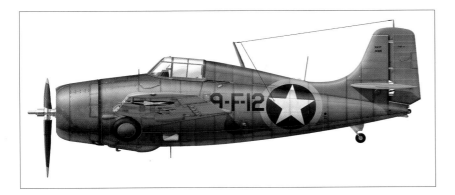

Black 9-F-12: F4F-4 of VF-9 during Operation *Torch*, November 1942. (Thierry Dekker)

Black 5: F4F-4 of VF-29 in the dark gull gray and insignia white Atlantic paint scheme, November 1943. (Thierry Dekker)

White MF-1: F4F-3 (tail designation shows F4F-4) of VMF-224 flown by Major R. Galer at Guadalcanal, September 1942. (Thierry Dekker)

White F28: F4F-4 of VF-11 "Sundowners" at Guadalcanal, May 1943. (Thierry Dekker)

machine guns and non-folding wings. The -3 went through a series of engine and cowling modifications during its service.

The F4F-3A used the Pratt & Whitney R1830-90 engine with the single-stage, two-speed supercharger. This version is distinguished by the lack of the two intercooler intakes inside the cowling. In its quest for fighter aircraft, Greece purchased 30 F4F-3As, which were shipped off in March 1941. However, before the shipment could arrive, the Germans overran Greece and the aircraft were turned over to the Royal Navy, who promptly christened them the Martlet III. These aircraft were assigned to No. 805 Squadron and were put into service in North Africa.

Next in the series was the F4F-4. The two major differences from the -3 series were the addition of two machine guns, for a total of six, and the installation of manually folding wings. The folding wings were a welcome change, lessening the aircraft's footprint so more could be stored on an aircraft carrier. The Wildcat's pilots did not receive the additional armament so warmly. The two additional guns made the aircraft heavier than the -3, with a consequential reduction in performance. Firing time was also now reduced, as each gun had less ammunition than before. Pilots generally preferred the longer firing time of four guns over the increased firepower of six. It was the F4F-3 and -4 that held the line in the Pacific against faster and more agile Japanese opposition.

The Wildcatfish was a prototype floatplane converted from a late-production F4F-3 Wildcat. Naval military planners were concerned about a possible shortage of carriers and airbases in the Pacific from which to operate aircraft, so the idea of fitting the Wildcat with Edo floats was conceived. It is also said that the Navy was impressed with the Japanese Imperial Navy's A6M2-N "Rufe" floatplane and hoped to emulate its performance. The prototype was first flown in February 1943, but its performance was disappointing. As it turned out, America was able to build aircraft carriers and airfields faster than anticipated and the Wildcatfish program became irrelevant.

When Grumman halted production of the F4F-4 to concentrate on their new Hellcat fighter, General Motors' aircraft division, Eastern Aircraft, was given the task of continuing Wildcat production in April 1942. Their first production Wildcat was designated the FM-1, which was essentially a Grumman F4F-4 whose armament had now been reduced back to the original four machine guns. Later, Eastern altered the design to become the FM-2. This version had a more powerful, lighter-weight engine than previous versions, making it the "hot rod" of the Wildcat family. The FM-2 can be distinguished by its shorter cowling and distinctly taller tail.

Designation		Characteristic	Notes
US Navy	**Fleet Air Arm**		
XF-4F-1		The first F4F was a biplane.	Design began in 1935, but never left the drawing board.
XF-4F-2		Monoplane with P&W R-1830-66 engine. Two cowl-mounted .30-cal. machine guns.	Lost out to the Brewster XF-2A-1 (Buffalo) in Navy trials in June 1938.
XF-4F-3		P&W R-1830-76 engine with two-stage, two-speed supercharger. Various large spinners used in an attempt to improve engine cooling.	US Navy decided to continue with the aircraft's development. One built.
F4F-3		Both P&W R-1830-76 and R-1830-86 engines used. Four .50-cal machine guns mounted in wings. Spinner deleted. Straight pitot tube and non-folding wings. Early production had two cowl flaps, late production had eight. Curtiss Electric cuffed prop.	The -86 engine is recognized by the two magnetos on top of the crankcase. First production contract awarded in August 1939. 285 built.
F4F-3P		F4F-3s with camera installations.	
F4F-3A	Martlet III	Production version of the XF-4F-6. Fitted with the P&W R-1830-90 engine with a single stage, two-speed supercharger. No intercooler air scoops inside the cowling. Two cowl flaps. Curtiss Electric cuffed prop. Non-folding wings.	95 built, 30 going to Greece in 1941. However, the shipment was diverted to Great Britain and became FAA Martlet IIIs.
G-36A	Martlet I	Wright R-1820-40 engine with no cowl flaps. Hamilton Standard Hydromatic prop. Armed with four 7.5mm Darn machine guns.	Originally a French order, but taken over by Great Britain when France was occupied. Not equipped for carrier operations. 91 built.
	Martlet II	Similar to F4F-3A, but with folding wings and three .50-cal. machine guns per wing.	First ten Martlet IIs had non-folding wings.
F4F-3S		Floatplane version with twin floats attached.	Named "Wildcatfish". First flight in February 1943. Performance was not satisfactory and design dropped. One built.
XF-4F-4		F4F-3 with hydraulically folding wings installed. Long pitot tube retained.	
F4F-4		Manually folding wings. Armament increased to three .50-cal. machine guns per wing. "L"-shaped pitot tube. R-1830-86 engines used. Eight cowl flaps. Curtiss Electric cuffed prop.	Developed from the Martlet II. 1,169 built.
F4F-4B	Martlet IV	An F4F-4, but with the Wright R-1820-40B engine with two cowl flaps and a Hamilton Standard Hydromatic prop.	
XF-4F-5		Wright R-1820-40 engine.	Test bed for the Wright engine as a possible alternative to the P&W. Only two built.
XF-4F-6		Fitted with the P&W R-1830-90 engine with a single-stage, two-speed supercharger.	Due to problems with the supercharger installation on the F3F, this was used as a test bed for the alternative engine/supercharger combination. Only one built.
XF-4F-7		Long-range reconnaissance version. No armament. Wings were non-folding and used as additional fuel tanks. Camera installed. Used the P&W R-1830-86 engine.	Only 21 built and delivered in 1942.
XF-4F-8		Test bed for the taller tail and rudder and the Wright R-1820-56 engine.	Would go into production as the FM-2.
FM-1	Martlet V/Wildcat V	Same as the F4F-4, but had only two .50-cal. machine guns per wing.	Built by the Eastern Aircraft division of the General Motors Corp. 839 built.
FM-2	Wildcat VI	Lightweight version of the F4F-4. Taller tail and rudder to counteract increased torque from engine. Two .50-cal. machine guns per wing. Used the Wright R-1820-56 engine with a single-stage, two-speed supercharger. Two cowl flaps. Curtiss Electric prop with Hamilton-style propellers.	Built by the Eastern Aircraft division of the General Motors Corp. Greater horsepower and lighter weight gave it better performance than earlier Wildcats. 4,737 built.

The Wildcat in detail

The FM-2

This section contains images of the FM-2 Wildcat located at the Palm Springs Air Museum in Palm Springs, California. This aircraft is in flyable condition.

While not in authentic markings, this aircraft has been restored to flying condition.

With the wings folded, note how the ailerons hinge upward.

The Wright Cyclone engine used on the FM-2. This had a single row of cylinders as opposed to the double row on the Pratt & Whitney engine on the F4F.

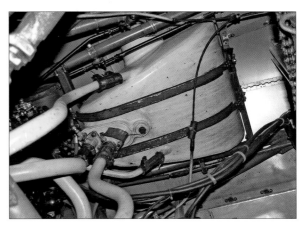

The engine oil tank located in the upper portion of the wheel well.

The center support for the landing gear.

The "bicycle chain" drive mechanism for operation of the landing gear.

Detail of the inner wheel hub. The hydraulic brake line attaches forward of the strut and runs along the backside of the strut into the wheel well.

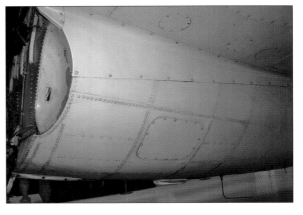

On the FM-2, the lower fuselage windows were not used and faired over.

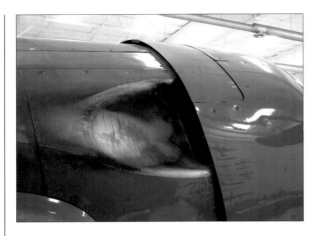

The exhaust arrangement on the FM-2 was much different to that of the F4F.

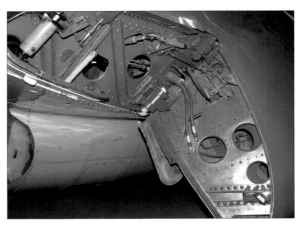

Interior detail of the wing-fold mechanism.

Rear portion of the folding wing interior.

Rear portion of the inner wing interior. The numerous holes in the structure help to lighten the airframe.

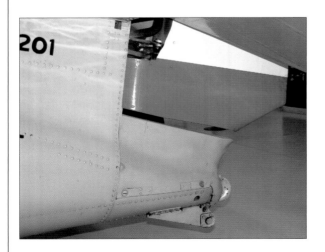

Details of the tail and rudder mechanism can be seen here.

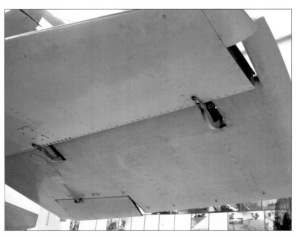

Details of the underside of the horizontal stabilizer.

The F4F-4

This section contains images of the F4F-4 Wildcat located at the San Diego Air & Space Museum in San Diego, California.

ABOVE The museum's F4F-4 sits atop a mock-up of an aircraft carrier's ready-room.

BELOW The markings are of Captain Marion Carl, USMC, who flew with VMF-223 at Guadalcanal in August 1942.

View of the wheel well interior. Note the chain drive for the landing gear retraction system.

Details of the aileron hinges. The hinges are quite prominent on the underside of the wing.

Vertical stabilizer of the F4F-4. A spring is used to keep tension on the antenna wire.

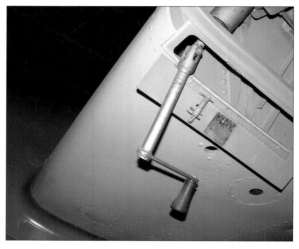

This handle would be turned to lock the wings in the extended position. When not in use, the handle folded up into the wing.

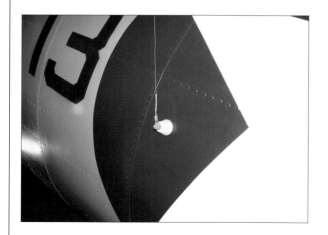

The antenna wire extended down and connected to the radio via an insulator on the left side of the fuselage.

Details of the sliding canopy. Note the raised rivets that covered much of the Wildcat.

The armored glass windshield is still intact in this aircraft. The gunsight has seen better days.

The cockpit is amazingly intact with most of the original components. The cockpit has the correct bronze green color.

Details of the rudder pedals. The control stick is missing the grip portion.

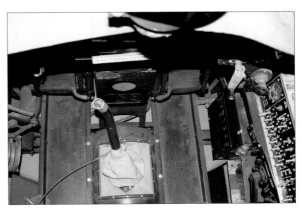

The Wildcat didn't have a cockpit floor. Instead, the pilot's feet rested on two foot troughs. The bottom of the cockpit was open to allow viewing through the two windows on the lower fuselage.

A good view of the left side of the cockpit. The two red handles at the bottom are for charging the machine guns. The black handle at the top right controls the arresting hook.

Details of the right rear of the cockpit. The green oxygen bottle can just be seen behind the seat.

Desert cat – Hasegawa's 1/72-scale Martlet III

Subject:	*Martlet Mk III*
Kit used:	*Hasegawa Martlet III (00694)*
Skill level:	*Intermediate*
Scale:	*1/72*
Additional detailing sets used:	*True Details Resin Seat (72411); Eduard F4F-4 Wildcat photo-etch set (72209)*
Markings:	*Kit decals*

The Hasegawa 1/72-scale Wildcat/Martlet series was first released in the mid-1990s. With this kit, Hasegawa took their usual approach of getting the most return for their mold investments. The parts Hasegawa provides are for the later F4F-4 variant with its folding wings, eight cowl flaps and six machine guns – all of which are incorrect for the Martlet III. Rather than give you the correct parts for the version shown on the box, Hasegawa has you do the work of converting the kit into the version you thought you were buying. Admittedly, it's not a great deal of work to make the necessary changes, but it is a little dishonest on Hasegawa's part to be advertising one thing on the box and then giving you something else inside.

The only real negative to the kit is the cockpit and wheel well detail. Essentially, there isn't any. The cockpit consists of a seat, stick, two raised side panels and an instrument panel decal. With the small cockpit opening and a closed canopy, there will not be much to see anyway. The wheel well is completely open, with nary a bulkhead in sight. These issues aside, the kit builds into a beautiful little rendition of the Fleet Air Arm's Martlet III.

Of the 1/72-scale Wildcats available, the Hasegawa one is the finest of the lot.

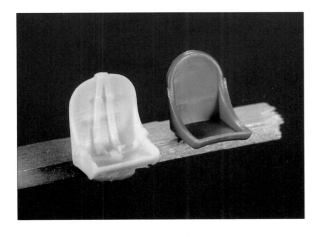

The True Details resin seat with harness is an improvement over the kit seat and adds some noticeable detail to the cockpit.

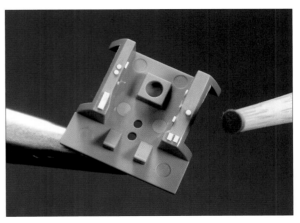

Pieces of punched and shaped styrene add some detail to an otherwise featureless cockpit. A piece of sandpaper glued to the end of a chopstick creates a sanding tool that can reach into tight spaces. A Waldron punch was used to make the sanding discs.

Cockpit and engine

Since I was going to have a closed canopy, I decided to keep the cockpit detailing to a minimum. First off, the cockpit floor had six prominent ejection-pin marks, two of which would be visible once it was assembled. These were removed by filling them with Mr Surfacer 500 and sanding them smooth, using a piece of sandpaper glued to the end of a chopstick. The True Details resin seat with harness replaced the kit seat, as this would improve this visible area of the cockpit.

Since the cockpit is so sparse, I wanted to create at least some detail, without going to the expense and effort of a resin cockpit or adding photo-etch parts. I decided to add various pieces of round and strip styrene to simulate the various controls. Using cockpit photos as a guide, pieces were punched out with a Waldron punch set or cut with a hobby knife to make knobs, panels and levers. This is a simple task and did not take very long to complete.

The cockpit was painted with Gunze Sangyo H302 Green, which is a good match for the intangible bronze green color that was used in the early F4F cockpits. The seat harness was brush painted with Tamiya XF-57 Buff, keeping

The cockpit color has been sprayed on. Early F4Fs used bronze green as their cockpit color. It is noticeably different to interior green, being darker and having a bluish tinge to it.

Ready for installation. Even with the additional cockpit detailing, it will be difficult to see much through the canopy. The two-piece engine is simple, but effective. Some ignition wires and crankcase detailing could really bring it to life.

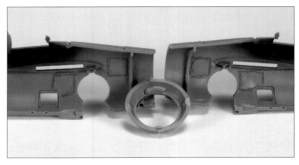

Several large ejection-pin marks around inside the fuselage and cowling. If not removed, they will be visible once the fuselage is complete. A Dremel tool with a grinding bit makes quick work of these.

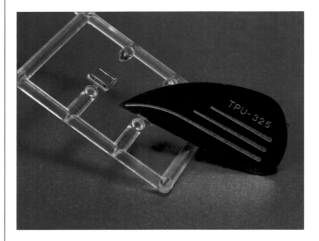

The two windows below the cockpit are installed prior to the fuselage halves going together. A micro saw does a nice job of removing clear parts from their sprue without damaging the part.

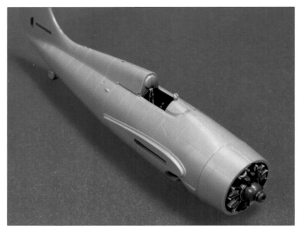

I should have installed the seat after the fuselage was together, as it would have been easier to paint the bulkhead and headrest. As it was, I carefully pulled the seat forward and masked it off.

The lines marked in red are those that need to be removed to convert the cowl flaps to the proper configuration.

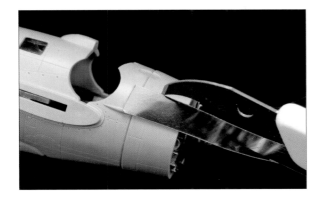

Once the new cowl flaps had been scribed, the panel line along the lower cowling had to be extended. Dymo tape is used as a guide for the scribing tool.

New cowl flaps for the Martlet. The previous cowl flaps, though gone, can still be seen through the clear CA glue.

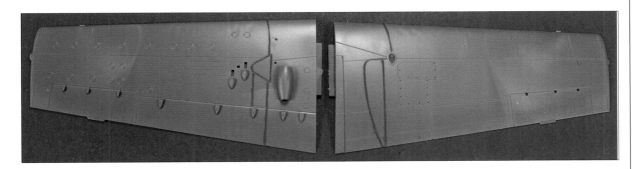

ABOVE The wing-fold lines on the upper and lower wings that needed to be removed were marked in red. The wing-fold housing on the upper wing also had to go.

BELOW The wing-fold housing has been removed with a chisel and the panel line rescribed. The outer wing guns are plugged with styrene rod. Notice the absence of the outer gun access panel. One less thing to do.

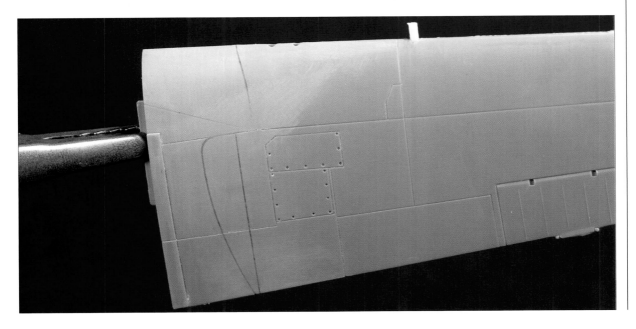

Styrene rod was used to fabricate the control shaft between the elevators.

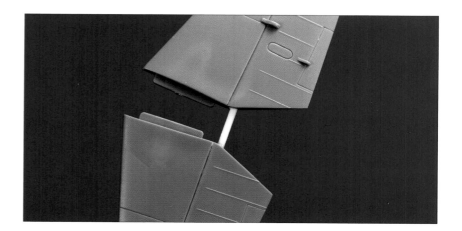

RIGHT A simple, but effective jig was used to ensure correct wing alignment.

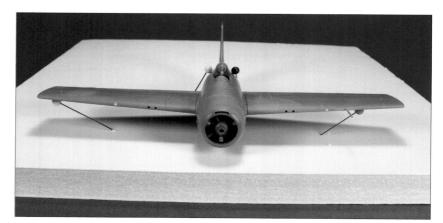

BELOW It's starting to look like an airplane. The slight gaps at the wing roots were removed using Mr Surfacer 500.

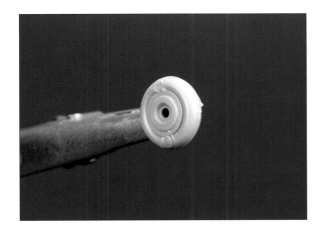

The kit wheels need a fair amount of clean-up.

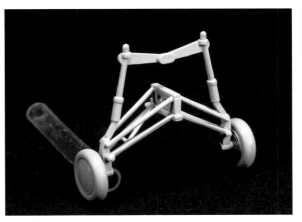

The Eduard photo-etch wheel hubs were installed on the inside hub. Two lightening holes were drilled into the center support for the landing gear.

the paint well thinned in order for it to flow on smoothly. I painted the instrument panel with Gunze Sangyo H77 Tire Black, hoping the color would be gray enough that the black instrument dials decal would contrast against it.

A light pinwash was done in the corners and crevices of the cockpit with a charcoal gray oil paint. As the aircraft being modeled was used in the desert, some MMP earth-colored pigment was mixed with Tamiya thinner and brushed in the corners of the cockpit and seat. A dab of Future acrylic floor wax was applied to the face of each instrument dial to give the effect of a glass lens.

Finally, the instrument hood was painted with Tamiya XF-63 German Black and the headrest sprayed with a Tamiya enamel mix of XF-10 Brown and XF-52 Earth.

The engine was assembled as part of the first step of the instruction sheet, along with the cockpit. Although it only consists of two parts, it is quite decent considering its small scale. The crankcase was sprayed with Gunze Sangyo H339 Engine Gray. The cylinders were then brush painted with Floquil Platinum Mist, thinned with Mr Color thinner to help avoid brush marks. The entire engine was then given a wash with a 50:50 mixture of charcoal gray and burnt sienna oils to bring out the detail and give it a used look.

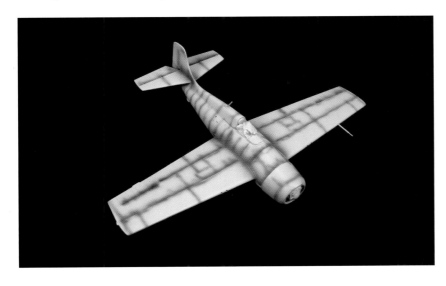

The model was pre-shaded with Tamiya XF-10 Flat Brown along panel lines, hatches and areas of shadow. No need for precision here, as it all adds to the weathered effect.

The canopy was masked and first painted with the bronze green color that would show through into the interior. Silly putty was used to mask the demarcation lines.

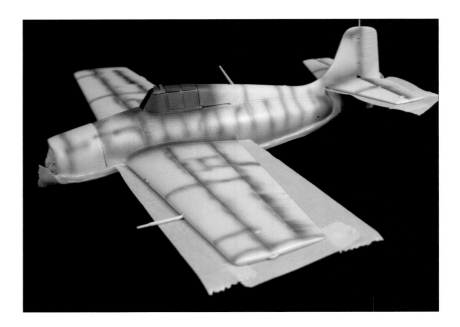

Just enough of the flat brown was allowed to show through for weathering. The silly putty does a superb job of masking between colors.

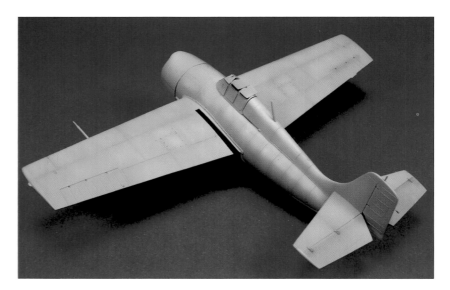

The end result of pre and post-shading. The brown pre-shade is just showing through, while the post-shading is subtle. Combined, they can give interest and depth to an otherwise monochromatic paint scheme.

The control surfaces were masked off using Tamiya tape.

I painted the two exhausts with Alclad II Jet Exhaust and a mix of black and brown oils was applied to the inside of the exhaust for some depth and color.

Fuselage

There are two large ejection-pin marks inside the landing gear bay. As there are no bulkheads provided, these marks would be visible through the landing gear openings if not removed. Therefore, they were filled in with several applications of Mr Surfacer 500 and sanded smooth. These would disappear entirely under a coat of paint.

Interior areas of the fuselage other than the cockpit were sprayed with Gunze Sangyo H61 IJN Gray. This is a good match for Grumman Gray, which was the color used by Grumman Aircraft for all fuselage interior surfaces, other than the cockpit.

The tow bar located underneath the tail was trimmed away from the fuselage, as this was not found on the Martlet III.

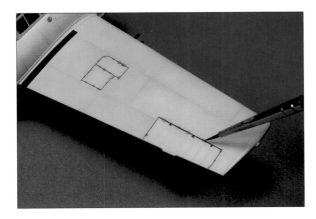

The oil mix was applied to the recesses with a pointed brush. Once dry, the excess could be removed with a cotton swab dampened with the Turpenoid, wiping in the direction of the airflow.

Faded, washed and nowhere to go. The final matt coat will tie everything together.

ABOVE After careful masking with Tamiya tape, the propeller hub was sprayed with Alclad Steel.

RIGHT Testor's Dullcote was used for the final matt finish.

The cockpit and engine assemblies were then trapped between the fuselage halves as they are glued together. The fuselage went together almost perfectly, with only a couple of spaces that needed a touch of thin cyanoacrylate (CA) glue to remedy small gaps.

The cowling is where you need to make the first modification to the kit to model the Martlet III. The kit's eight cowl flaps (four per side) need to be reduced down to two, large flaps. The instructions show you which of the existing cowl lines to remove. The engraved lines for the cowl flaps were first filled in with CA glue and, once dry, were sanded down with 400-, then 600-grit sandpaper. Now the new cowl flaps could be rescribed. Dymo tape was laid out as a guide for the outline of the new cowl flaps and the new lines made with my favorite scribing tool, a compass needle in a pin vise.

Wings

The engraved wing-fold lines also need to be removed in order to model the Martlet III version. The instructions clearly show which lines to remove on the upper and lower wings. To help avoid filling in the wrong lines, areas that needed to be removed were marked in red pencil for easy identification. The lines were again removed by the method of filling with CA glue and sanding them smooth. The wing-fold hinge housing on the upper wing also needs to be deleted. This was done with a small chisel and then sanded flush with the wing. Once the corrections had been made, some minor rescribing of panel lines was carried out.

The outer wing guns had to be deleted, as the Martlet III only had two guns per wing. The kit supplies plastic inserts for the gun ports, but I used a piece of styrene rod, as it fitted the opening more closely. Once the glue had dried, the end of the rod was snipped off and sanded flush with the leading edge of the wing. To better model the wing guns, the kit's machine guns were replaced with .032in. brass tubing, cut to length with a hobby knife blade. Hasegawa saves you the trouble of removing the outer wing gun-access panels, as they did not mold them onto the upper wing.

The kit does not include the connecting shaft between the two elevators that runs through the rudder. This was fabricated from .035in. styrene rod and a hole was drilled into the inside portion of each elevator for the rod to fit into. The rod was then glued into one elevator and the stabilizer glued into position. The other end of the rod was trimmed down and test fitted until the remaining stabilizer fit properly against the fuselage.

LEFT Stretched sprue was used to make the wire antennas. They were attached to the radio masts using CA glue.

BELOW The Martlet III is the British version of the F4F-3A Wildcat.

The Pratt & Whitney R-1830-90 engine used in the Martlet III was not equipped with supercharger intercoolers; therefore it did not have the dual air scoops inside the cowling.

ABOVE Fabric-covered control surfaces tended to fade faster and in a different manner to metal-painted surfaces.

BELOW Four guns is all the Martlet III needed. The later six-gun versions of the F4F would lead to pilot complaints of excessive weight and fewer rounds per gun.

After the wings were attached, there was a slight gap at the wing root that was filled with Mr Surfacer 500. After the Mr Surfacer 500 was allowed to dry, it was smoothed out with a cotton swab dampened with Mr Colour Thinner. This made for a smooth wing root with the appearance of a seam line.

The front cowling is attached in this step and the instructions call for installing the two intercooler intakes inside the cowling. However, the intercoolers were not used on the Martlet III engine, so these should be left off.

To help with getting the proper wing alignment, a simple jig was made from ½in. foam board and straight pins. The fuselage was pinned into place, taking measurements on each side to make sure that it was perpendicular to the board's surface. The wings were then attached and supported by two straight pins. The pins could be easily moved up and down to reposition the wings as needed to get the proper angles. Measurements were taken off each wing to ensure everything was in alignment. Once dry, the alignment came out spot-on.

Landing gear

I had originally planned to use the True Details resin wheels; however, they appeared undersized compared to the kit wheels, so the kit wheels it was.

The landing gear struts Nos. B4 and B12 are quite delicate and require careful handling during removal from their sprues and clean-up. In fact, in my original Martlet III kit, part No. B12 arrived crushed beyond repair, causing me to have to invest in another kit.

I used the Eduard photo-etch interior wheel hubs to dress up this otherwise plain area. In order to give myself some working time to position the photo-etch parts over the wheel hub, Future floor wax was used as an adhesive. Future allows more working time than CA glue, while still providing a decent bond for non-load-bearing photo-etch parts.

Two .062in. lightening holes were drilled into the center support of part No. B12, then the wheel well area and the upper portion of the strut assembly was painted Grumman Gray.

The landing gear assembly did not fit properly into the wheel well when I went to install it. The fairing at the base of the struts refused to sit flush with the bottom of the fuselage. It was necessary to trim the ends of the struts to shorten them, allowing the fairing to sit flush.

The two landing gear doors fit well, but unfortunately don't fit in the proper position. They sit almost vertical, instead of diagonally as they should.

Painting and decals

There has been plenty of debate about the true colors of No. 805 Squadron's aircraft in North Africa. The most often cited color schemes are overall light gray, middle stone over azure blue or middle stone/dark earth over azure blue. It is reasonable to conclude that all of these schemes may have been found at one time or another. Photos show "Black X" as most likely being middle stone over azure blue, so that's what I went with.

First the model was pre-shaded with Tamiya XF-10 Flat Brown, as this seemed like a good pre-shade base for the colors to follow. The underside surfaces were painted with MisterKit MKRAF09 Azure Blue, making sure the pre-shading showed through. White was then added to the Azure Blue to lighten it and the mix thinned even more. It was sprayed in a random pattern on the lower surfaces to create some variation in the color. I try to avoid simply filling in the centers of panels so I don't end up with the "quilted" look. Silly putty was rolled up and used for masking the demarcation line between the upper and lower colors. Upper surfaces were then painted with MisterKit MKRAF08 Middle Stone. As before, the paint was sprayed on in thin coats to allow the pre-shading to show through. The Middle Stone was then lightened with a little white, thinned and randomly sprayed on. A light coat of Middle Stone was then sprayed over the surface to blend the colors together. The upper fabric control surfaces were weathered further using a mix of Middle Stone, MKRAF26 White and some MKRAF16 Sky Gray, as they would fade quicker and differently than the metal surfaces.

The engraved lines around control surfaces and hatches were given a pin wash of charcoal gray and white oil mix. I wanted to avoid a color that was too dark, as it might look too stark against the Middle Stone in this scale. All of the other panel lines were pin washed with a mix of raw sienna, white and raw umber oils. Again, avoiding a color that would contrast too much with the airframe colors.

The canopy was masked with the Eduard vinyl masks and then sprayed with the cockpit interior color that would show through on the inside. Over that was sprayed the Middle Stone. The wing walk strips were painted with Tamiya XF-69 NATO Black. The model was then sprayed with several coats of Future in preparation for decals.

The kit decals were in perfect register and had a muted color to them that worked well with the weathered finish of the model. The decals went down smoothly and conformed perfectly using the Microscale system of Micro-Set and Micro-Sol. Once the decals were dry, they were wiped down with warm water to remove any traces of the Microscale solutions. The previously used panel line oil wash was applied over the decals to fill the panel lines and to weather them a bit more. A coating of Testor's Dullcote was applied to the entire model to matt down the finish. Some paint wear was simulated with a dark gray artist's pencil and the navigation lights were painted with Gunze Sangyo H90 Clear Red and H94 Clear Green, after an initial coat of silver. Finally, MMP pigments were used for the exhaust and gun stains and a little tire weathering.

The finishing touch was to fashion the wire antennas from stretched sprue.

Martlet IIIs were assigned to No. 805 Squadron of the Fleet Air Arm and took part in operations in North Africa.

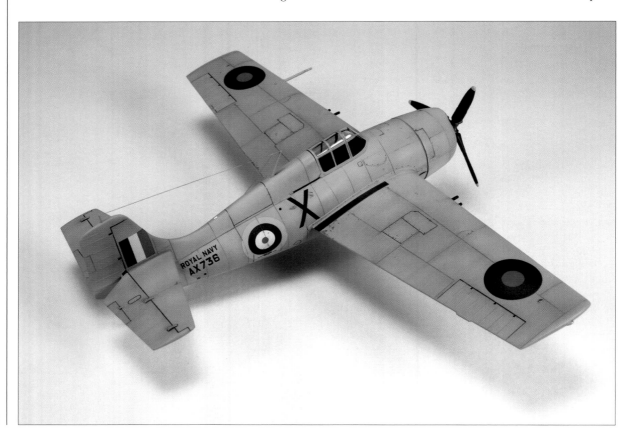

McCuskey's Midway ride – converting Tamiya's 1/48-scale F4F-4 to the F4F-3 Wildcat

Subject:	*Gruman F4F-3 Wildcat*
Kit used:	*Tamiya F4F-4 Wildcat (61034)*
Skill level:	*Advanced*
Scale:	*1/48*
Additional detailing sets used:	*Eduard Wildcat photo-etch set (EDU49246); Part F4F Wildcat photo-etch set (S48-027); Ultracast F4F Wildcat seats (early war harness) (48055); Cutting Edge navigation lights (CEC48164); parts from the JPS F4F-3 conversion set (JPS016); Quickboost B-25B .50-cal. gun barrels (QB48022); Cutting Edge F4F flying control surfaces (CEC48230); Eduard F4F Wildcat painting mask (EX092); Cutting Edge USN Mk 8 gunsight (CEC48156)*
Markings:	*Yellow Wings Decals U.S. national insignia (YWD48005); Super Scale decals F4F-3 Wildcats (481032); Tally Ho! Wildcat national insignia paint masks (P48027)*

If you want to build a Wildcat in 1/48 scale, Tamiya's F4F-4 Wildcat kit is currently the only game in town. Fortunately, it's a very good game. Having been first released in 1994, it still holds up very well and is simple to build. The only real issues the kit has are the oversized raised rivets and the solid cockpit floor, both of which can be easily corrected.

Lt. E. Scott McCuskey's F4F-3 from the USS *Yorktown*, May 1942.

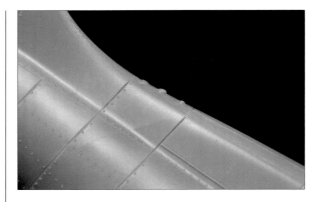

The navigation lights on the spine were removed and would be replaced with a single clear lens for the F4F-3.

To fashion the elevator hinges, two holes were carefully drilled into the center of the hinge. Then a hobby knife and a round file were used to open up and shape the hole.

The connecting shaft between the two elevators was made from .05in. styrene rod.

Repositioned control surfaces and tailwheel add a lot to the personality and interest of a finished model. The tailwheel was removed with a micro saw, and strengthened with a piece of .02in. brass wire.

The cockpit floor area outlined in red should be removed to correctly model the Wildcat's interior.

Rub 'n Buff was used to add some wear to the cockpit floor and seat. This was done using a dry brush technique with a small, stiff brush.

The Eduard Color photo-etch is all the kit cockpit needs to really set it off. Additional detailing around the cockpit for wiring and control linkages was done using .01in. and .015in. metal rod and solder wire.

Some of the pre-painted Eduard parts are painted in the incorrect interior green color. These parts were sprayed with light coats of the Model Master color until the correct shade was reached. To recover any lost lettering and detail, a fine brush dipped in Tamiya thinner was run over the areas to remove the paint.

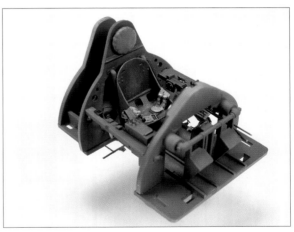

The early F4F-3's seats were only equipped with a lap belt. I used the Ultracast resin seat with the early war harness. The lap belt was painted with Tamiya XF-57 Buff and then given a brown oil wash.

I had originally planned on using the Just Plane Stuff F4F-3/3A Wildcat conversion set to backdate the kit. This set contains a resin wing, several cowlings, intercoolers with intakes and an engine crankcase. However, the quality of the molding on my sample was rather disappointing and it was apparent that quite a bit of work was going to be needed to bring it up to an acceptable level. I decided my time would be better spent backdating the kit wing to the F4F-3 version, as I would end up with a more detailed wing and a much better fit. As it was, I only ended up using a few parts out of the conversion kit.

Mix some photo-etch, a couple of resin parts and a dash of scratch-building and you end up with a very nice cockpit.

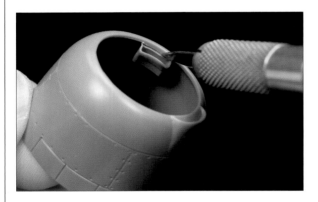

The kit intakes were removed by scribing with a hobby knife along the edge of the intake and cowling until they could be pulled out. Once removed, sandpaper and a file were used to sand flush the inner cowl rim.

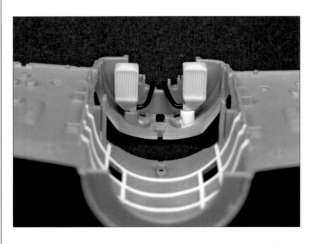

A second intercooler base was made from styrene tubing. The resin intercoolers fit perfectly when installed. The interior framing of the lower fuselage was replicated with strip styrene.

Fuselage and horizontal stabilizers

I didn't want to keep the raised rivets, so the first order of business was to sand them off the fuselage and wings. I still wanted some rivet detail, so using a Rosie the Riveter tool and a detailed drawing, rivets were placed on the fuselage, wings and tail in all of the appropriate places. The rivets this tool makes are quite subtle, just how they should be in 1/48 scale. A missing fuel tank filler hatch was also scribed onto the left side of the fuselage.

Tamiya calls for their own Tamiya paint mix of interior green (two parts XF-3 Flat Yellow to one part XF-5 Flat Green) to be used for the cockpit. However, the earlier F4F-3 cockpits were painted bronze green. Model Master's Euro I Dark Green acrylic is a good match for this color and was applied to the cockpit sidewalls.

The rudder and horizontal stabilizers are also installed in the first step of the instruction sheet. I wanted to have both of them deflected, which would be easy enough as the rudder is molded separately, but would take some surgery for the one-piece horizontal stabilizer.

The elevators were carefully cut away until only the four hinges were left attached to the stabilizer. A hole was then drilled in the center of each hinge and filed to shape. This had to be done very carefully, as the hinges were not hanging on by much at this point. A groove was then cut into the trailing edge of the stabilizer for the leading edge of the elevators to fit into. First, a deep line was scribed down the middle of the trailing edge as a starting point. The scraping began with a curved hobby knife blade and a chisel with a rounded blade. Work continued until the proper shape and depth was achieved. It was important to work slowly and test fit often to avoid removing any more plastic than necessary. The Cutting Edge resin elevators were then CA glued onto the stabilizer in an upward deflected position. While the kit elevator looked every bit as good as the resin replacement, using the resin part saved the work of having to reshape the kit elevator's leading edge.

Detailing the cockpit

The kit's cockpit is very respectable and there isn't too much gained by replacing it with a resin cockpit. What can improve the cockpit is some Eduard photo-etch and a bit of scratch-building. Its only shortcomings are the solid floor and frumpy looking seat. The actual cockpit floor was open on the sides to permit viewing through the lower fuselage windows. This is easy enough to remedy by using a micro saw and scriber to remove the offending portions of the floor.

The horizontal bar on the rear bulkhead over the seat needs to be removed, as it was not found on the early F4F-3s. Removing the bar without doing damage

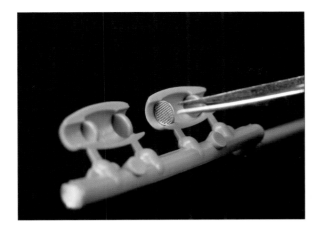

Photo-etch parts were attached to the oil coolers.

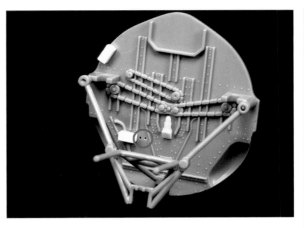

A few scratch-built items were added and two small holes were drilled into the wheel well bulkhead for the installation of the brake lines.

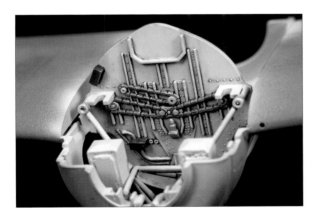

The chains and various parts were brush painted after the firewall was set in place.

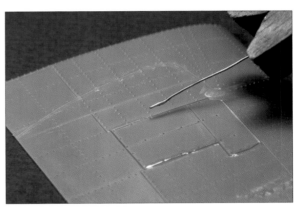

A piece of wire held in a clothes' pin is used as an applicator for CA glue.

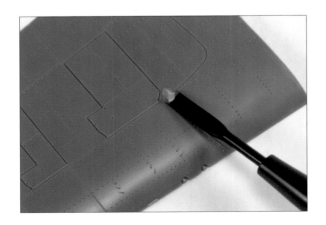

The wing-fold hinge blister on the upper wing is removed with a wide chisel blade.

After the first round of filling panel lines and sanding, you can see the effect on the upper wing. Next comes the rescribing and rivet replacement. Dark gray paint was sprayed on to show any imperfections.

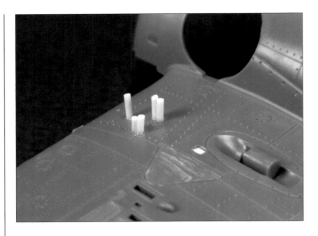

Holes too big for CA glue to handle were first stuffed with styrene.

The panel lines are rescribed with a compass needle held in a pin vise. Dymo tape makes a great straight edge.

to surrounding detail is difficult because of the tight space. To work around this, the rear bulkhead was cut in half just below the line of rivets underneath the headrest using a micro saw. Now the bar could be sanded off without the risk of removing surrounding detail and the two pieces were reattached.

The knobs on the photo-etch levers were made from dabs of white glue applied with a toothpick. Many of the photo-etch parts in the cockpit were attached using Future, rather than CA glue.

Cutting Edge's impressive little Mk 8 resin gunsight was used to replace the generic-looking kit sight.

Cockpit painting

As with the cockpit sidewalls, the cockpit was painted with Model Master's Euro I Dark Green acrylic. This was then lightened with Model Master RAF Interior Green with some additional thinner added for some highlights and then darkened with Model Master Scale Black for shadows.

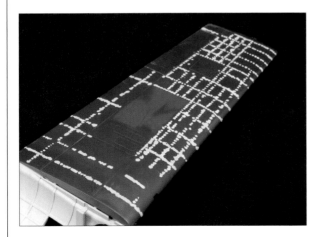

The rivet holes in the wing were considerably larger than the holes made by the Rosie the Riveter tool. In order to keep the rivet appearance consistent, I filled in the wing rivet holes with Mr Surfacer 500 and replaced them with the Rosie tool. This turned out to be a very tedious process.

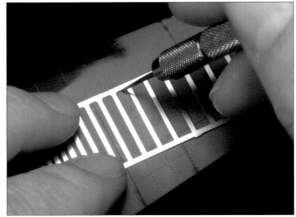

A collection of templates in various shapes and sizes is a must for rescribing surface details. Here the access panels are being done.

The Quickboost .5-cal. machine-gun barrels add some very realistic detail to the kit.

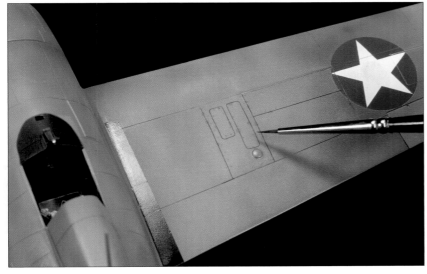

The small bulge located behind the machine-gun panels was made from a disc of .16in. styrene. It was sanded around the edges to give it the correct domed shape. Stretched sprue was used to make the hinges for the machine-gun and flotation bag access panels. A pin wash is being applied here.

The instruments were painted with Tamiya XF-1 Flat Black enamel. Using enamel paint over an acrylic to paint details allows you to easily correct any mistakes by touching up with enamel thinner, as this won't affect the acrylic paint underneath.

Instruments were given a drybrushing of charcoal gray and white oil paint mix. A wash of dark gray enamel was used in the cockpit in the corners to accent shadows.

The instrument panel was masked off to protect the instrument dial faces and a mix of Pollyscale matt and satin varnish was used on the cockpit as the final coat.

Scratch-built detail was added to the kit engine and Eduard photo-etch ignition wires were used for the rear row of cylinders.

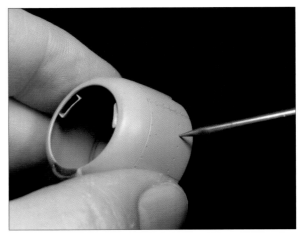

To improve the surface detail, the cowling attachment points were detailed with the MDC rivet tool.

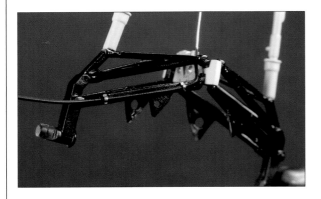

To make the strut attachment points for the brake lines, .01 in. solder wire was flattened with the handle of a hobby knife and cut to length. These were then formed around the wire and CA-glued into place.

Once the landing gear assembly was in place, the ends of the brake lines were carefully inserted into the drilled holes in the bulkhead, using a pair of tweezers.

This is why it's called the Grumman Iron Works. Never having much success with filing the bottoms of tires, I've gone to using heat to get the weighted look. By placing the model on an iron or frying pan and using low heat, the tires can be melted to the proper level with a nice, even bottom. This must be done slowly, under a watchful eye.

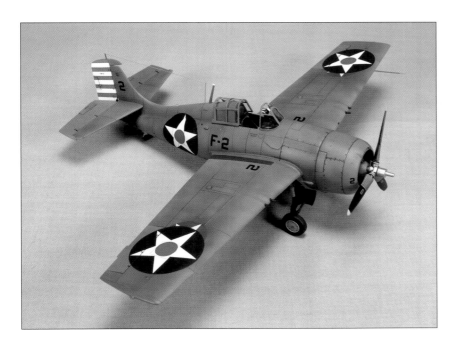

The upper blue-gray colour was faded by adding some white to the mix and randomly spraying over the surfaces.

Once the cockpit painting was complete, it was installed through the fuselage bottom and glued into place. I deviated from the instructions here by not attaching the wheel well bulkhead to the cockpit assembly. The bulkhead was later attached to the lower wing, as this provided a better fit and fewer seam issues inside the wheel well.

Lower wing assembly

The F4F-3 had two intercoolers located behind the engine inside the wheel well. However, the F4F-4, which the Tamiya kit is based on, was equipped with only one. So a matching base for the second intercooler was made from .128in. styrene tube. As the kit only supplies a single intercooler, the two resin intercoolers from the JPS set were used in its place. The ducting coming off the JPS intercoolers was too short, so it was cut off and replaced with .045in. insulated wire, which was glued in place and bent to the correct shape.

The cuffed portion of the prop was painted with Alclad Steel and the hub painted in Alclad Aluminum. This was done to provide some contrast between the two parts.

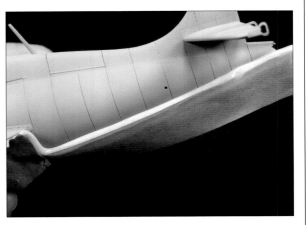

Silly putty was rolled up to make a mask for the demarcation lines between the two exterior colors.

The original national insignia on the upper wing was painted on by using Tally Ho! paint masks.

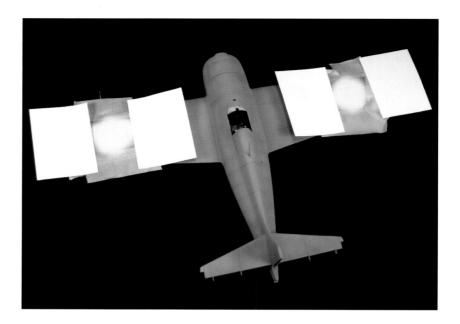

An oil wash of burnt umber and charcoal gray was used inside the wheel well. With all of the gearing, plumbing, engine, etc., I imagine this was a rather dirty environment. When applying an oil wash without a clear coat, it allows the oils to stain the matt surface of the paint, enhancing the weathering effect. The wash was also done on the intercoolers to highlight the grille faces. Any high points were then dry brushed with a mix of titanium white and Davy's gray oils, keeping it subtle so that there is little perception that it's there.

Converting the wing to an F4F-3

On the upper wing, the first order of business was to fill in all of the wing-fold and machine-gun access panel lines with CA glue. The machine-gun access panels sat higher than the wing's surface and were sanded flush. For the lower wing, the holes for the drop tanks, outer machine-gun ejection chutes and the hole for the pitot tube were filled in. These holes were too large for CA glue alone to fill, so they were first filled with bits of styrene and sanded down. Any remaining gaps could then be filled with CA glue.

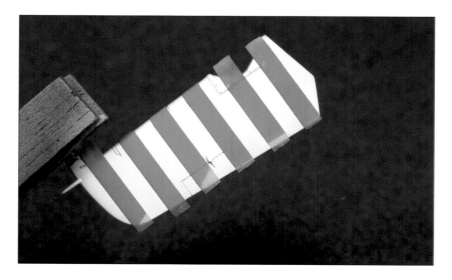

Rather than use the kit decals, the red and white stripes on the rudder were painted on. The rudder was first painted white, then strips of Tamiya tape were cut to the proper width and laid over the rudder to paint the red stripes.

The panel lines on the wings were rescribed using a compass point inserted into a pin vise, with Dymo tape providing a straight edge on which to scribe. After brushing out the groove, Tamiya thin cement was lightly applied along the scribed line. This dissolves any tiny rough spots and smoothes out the groove. A metal template was used to rescribe the machine-gun and flotation bag access panels.

All of the gun ports were filled in with CA glue and the four inner ports were then drilled out with a .055in. drill. Having done this, new machine-gun barrels would be needed. Quickboost makes a variety of resin gun barrels and their .50-cal. barrel set for the Accurate Miniatures B-25B kit fit the bill nicely. Tamiya has the guns incorrectly positioned along the midpoint of the leading edge of the wing, while they are actually located slightly above midpoint. A piece of styrene strip had been glued onto the inside bottom wing as a foundation for the resin Quickboost .50-cal. machine-gun barrels to rest against. The barrels were painted black and then rubbed down with silver Rub 'n Buff to give them a metallic look. They were then trimmed to the proper length and CA-glued against the styrene block.

Before being equipped with folding wings, the Wildcat used a straight pitot tube located on the leading edge of the port wing. This was fabricated from .025in. and .012in. telescoping metal tubing. A hole was drilled into the leading edge and the tube CA-glued into place.

Engine

The version of the engine that comes with the Tamiya kit is the Pratt & Whitney R-1830-86, which is correct for the F4F-4. However, the F4F-3 used the R-1830-76 engine, which does not have the two magnetos atop the crankcase. Fortunately, the crankcase comes as a separate piece, so the JPS resin crankcase was used, as it was the correct configuration with a single magneto. I rebuilt the magneto by filing it down and adding details made from styrene.

Some additional detailing was done to the resin crankcase by adding bolt-heads around the prop shaft using a .018in. punch and .016in. sheet styrene.

The JPS intercooler intakes were used to replace the kit intakes. The kit's intakes looked good from the front, but they only extended back about ¼in. from the edge of the cowl opening. The resin intakes had the correct ducting that runs between the cylinder heads and cowling interior. Once the kit intakes had been removed, the JPS intercooler intakes were glued in place. White glue, with its slow drying time, was used to hold the part in place while they were correctly positioned. Then CA glue was applied around the edges of the intakes to set them in place.

The kit cowling comes with four cowl flaps, while the F4F-3 used only two cowl flaps. To make the new cowl flaps, portions of the engraved cowl flaps lines were filled in with CA glue and sanded smooth. The new cowl flaps' lines were then scribed to the correct shape for the two flaps.

The engine crankcase was painted Gunze Sangyo H337 Grayish Blue and the cylinders with Tamiya XF-16 Aluminum enamel. The ignition wires were painted with Tamiya XF-9 Hull Red, and silver enamel was used to touch-up the crankcase boltheads.

Lastly, the engine was then given a wash of a black/brown mix of Tamiya enamels.

Landing gear

The rear supports for the landing-gear doors are missing the two lightening holes, so these were drilled through to create the holes. I wanted to include the hydraulic brake lines, since these are quite noticeable inside the wheel well. .02in. insulated wire was used for the lines, removing the insulation in places to represent the metal tubing portion of the brake lines. Small pieces of the insulation were then slid back on the wire to represent the hose connectors.

There is some question as to whether Lt. McCuskey actually flew a -3 or -4 Wildcat at Midway and if he would have had the six kill markings at the time.

Painting and decals for the F4F-3

The model was first pre-shaded with Tamiya XF-1 Flat Black. A mix of three parts Tamiya XF-18 Medium Blue and one part XF-2 White was sprayed on for the upper blue-gray color, allowing some of the pre-shading to show through. Some white was then added to the mix to lighten the color and it was thinned out even more. This was randomly misted onto the upper color to create a weathered effect. The fabric control surfaces were further weathered by a bit more white and some gray added to the previous mix. There is no science as to how much or what color to add for weathering effects, just whatever looks good to you. The lower surfaces were painted light gray, a mix of one part Tamiya XF-2 White and two parts XF-19 Sky Gray. Grumman painted the fuselage interior surfaces, other than the cockpit, in their proprietary color of Grumman Gray. This consisted of a mix of three parts Tamiya XF-2 White, one part XF-19 Sky Gray and one part XF-12 IJN Gray.

The smaller, original national insignia on the upper wings were painted using the Tally Ho! vinyl masks. Since a decal would be going over this, painting the insignia would help avoid the possible outline a decal might leave in the overlying decal. Gunze Sangyo H21 Off-White was used to give the star a slightly weathered look that would contrast with the more recently painted larger insignia.

Super Scale and Yellow Wing decals were applied using Micro-Sol. Areas where decals were to go were first sprayed with Future to provide a smooth surface for the decal to avoid silvering.

A mix of 50:50 turpentine and oil-based stain varnish was mixed for the final matt coat. I like this formula as it provides a very nice finish, with just a hint of a satiny look. The downside is that it is quite odorous (use in a well-ventilated area) and isn't quite as convenient as an out-of-the-bottle finish. It also takes about six hours to dry completely.

LEFT The kit captures the complex appearance of the landing gear.

BELOW The oversize national insignia markings were applied shortly after the start of hostilities as an aid in identifying US aircraft.

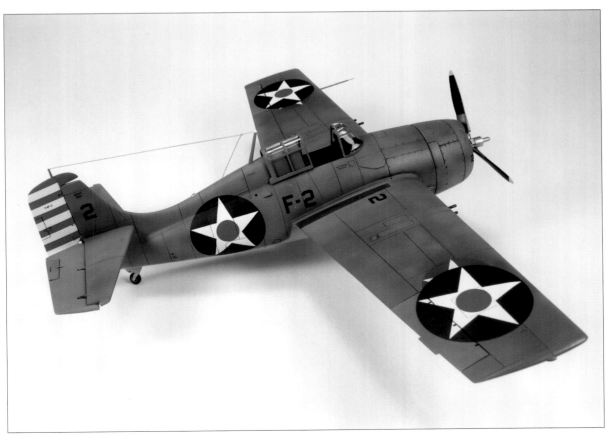

ABOVE **Grumman's** squat little fighter held the line against the Japanese forces in the Pacific in the early days of the war.

BELOW The freshly painted oversized national insignia contrasts nicely with the weathered finish of the paint.

Mixed-breed cat — using Tamiya's 1/48-scale F4F-4 Wildcat to improve the Sword 1/48-scale FM-2

Subject:	*Eastern Aircraft FM-2 Wildcat*
Kits used:	*Tamiya F4F-4 Wildcat (61034); Sword FM-2 Wildcat (48005)*
Skill level:	*Advanced*
Scale:	*1/48*
Additional detailing sets used:	*Ultracast resin seat (48029); KMC Resin Wright R-1820-56 engine (48-5077); Cutting Edge Resin Mk 8 gunsight (48156); Cutting Edge Resin FM-2 propeller and spinners (CEC48404); Eduard F4F Wildcat canopy mask (61034)*
Markings:	*Techmod Decals FM-2 Wildcat (48050); Mike Grant instrument dial faces (CKP048); Archers Fine Transfers German information placards (AR35215)*

The Sword FM-2 kit is currently the only kit available of this aircraft in 1/48 scale. No one will confuse this kit with the Tamiya Wildcat. Even though the Sword FM-2 is a so-called "limited-run" kit, the parts have the look of coming from very tired molds and most have varying amounts of flash on them. Surface detail consists of only shallow panel lines and a few access doors. There

An FM-2 from Composite Squadron Thirteen. It operated in the Atlantic in the anti-submarine role.

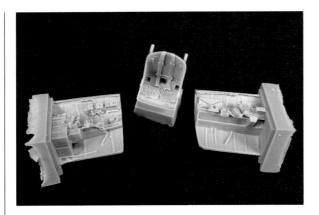

The Sword kit contains a three-piece resin cockpit. The seat, while nicely molded, was so thin in places that it literally crumbled when I tried to remove it from its casting block.

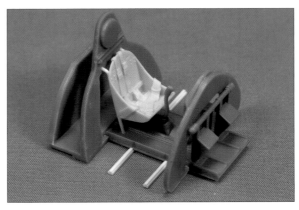

The Ultracast resin seat and a little scratch-building add some detail to the otherwise bland kit cockpit. The center console and rudder pedals from the Tamiya kit were also used.

Instant dials. Mike Grant instrument dial face decals were used on the instrument panel. These were punched from their sheet using the Waldron punch set.

The Sword resin cockpit is a little rough, but doesn't look bad through a closed canopy. The cockpit floor is incorrect in that it is molded solid. The sides of the floor were cut out using a Hasegawa scriber.

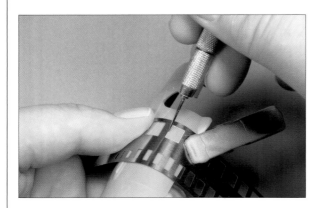

The two fuselage bottom windows were not used on the FM-2 and were faired over. The kit is missing this detail, so the outlines of the windows were scribed on using a metal template and a compass needle.

The Tamiya wheel well bulkhead and landing gear are much more detailed than the kit parts. The rear portion of the KMC engine has also been installed.

is no rivet detail anywhere on the model, which may or may not be to your liking. There are no locating pins and the plastic is rather thick compared to other kits. The propeller is incorrectly shaped and the kit contains a very peculiar-looking representation of the Wright 1820-56 engine. The plastic had an odd, rather gritty texture to it. I tried washing the parts in warm water and soap in an effort to remove any surface contaminants, but the odd texture remained. A buffing with a 4,000-grit Micro-Mesh cloth eventually smoothed out the surface.

In order to make up for the many deficiencies of the Sword kit, I decided to use various parts from the Tamiya Wildcat kit. As it turned out, the final product was more Tamiya than Sword.

Cockpit

The Sword kit provides a three-piece resin cockpit. Whenever you use a resin cockpit that includes sidewalls, the sides of the kit fuselage will typically need to be thinned down to get a better scale thickness once the resin sidewalls are attached. The sidewalls were cut from their casting blocks and glued into place using an epoxy cement. Epoxy was used primarily for the increased working time over CA glue to assure a proper fit. The Ultracast resin seat with its molded-on harness was used, as it was an improvement over the kit's resin seat. The Ultracast seat is without seat supports, so new ones were made from .025in. styrene rod by cutting them to the correct length and bending them to shape. Lastly, the instrument hood was sanded down to a more appropriate scale thickness.

The kit didn't include a gunsight, so I used the Cutting Edge resin Mk 8 gunsight. Once the sight was painted and attached to the instrument hood, the gunsight lens was scribed out of clear acetate, using a metal template as a scribing guide. The lens was buffed with plastic polish to remove any small scratches and attached to the sight with a small amount of Microscale Kristal Klear.

Unlike Grumman, Eastern Aircraft used interior green in their cockpits, so I painted the cockpit with Gunze Sangyo H58 Interior Green and picked out the details with Tamiya enamels. Then a very light dry brushing was applied, using a mix of white, sap green and Davy's gray oils. The instrument panel hood was painted with Gunze Sangyo H77 Tire Black. Some light paint chipping was done with a silver-gray artist's pencil. Finally, the cockpit was finished off with a 50:50 mix of Pollyscale acrylic Satin (404103) and Flat (404106).

Fuselage

The Sword fuselage was used for this build, as it had the taller tail, shorter cowling and different exhaust arrangement that was characteristic of the FM-2.

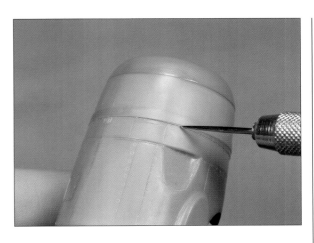

A missing panel line was scribed around the cowling, just in front of the cowl flaps. This was done using thin, flexible vinyl tape and a compass point in a pin vise.

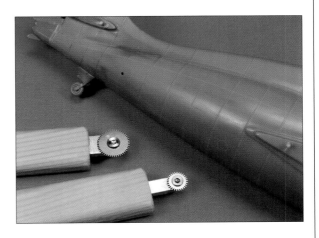

Rosie the Riveter was used to create the rivet detail along the fuselage.

Some fastener detail around the cowling was added with the use of a beading tool.

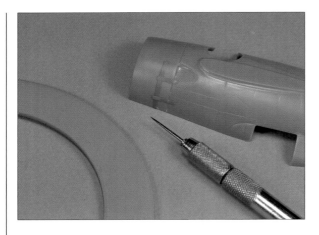

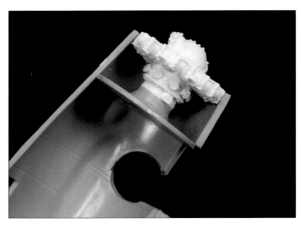

The cowl flaps on the kit were the wrong shape. They were filled with CA glue and sanded smooth. Then flexible vinyl tape and a scriber were used to create the correct cowl flaps.

The kit's engine mount had to be sanded down to accommodate the KMC engine. The KMC engine was actually a better fit inside the cowling than the kit engine.

The KMC engine builds into a nice replica of the Wright radial used on the FM-2.

The Cutting Edge FM-2 propeller was used to replace the poorly shaped kit prop.

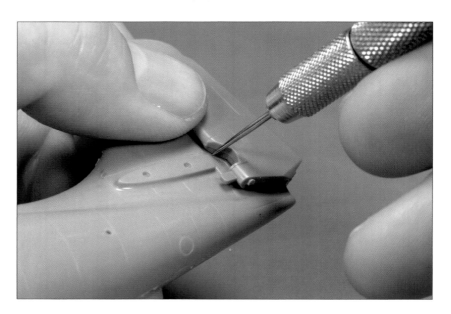

An opening in the kit rudder is prepared, using the Tamiya rudder as a scribing template.

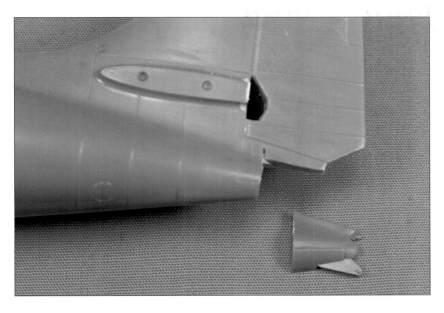

The tail of the Tamiya fuselage was grafted onto the Sword fuselage to provide the missing detail.

The Tamiya wheel well bulkhead contained much more detail than the Sword kit's part, so I decided to use it instead. It took a fair amount of sanding and test-fitting, but once the fuselage halves were glued together, the fit turned out to be quite good.

To add some interest to the rather plain Sword fuselage, rivets on the fuselage were made with a Rosie the Riveter tool. While not quite the same size as the rivets on the Tamiya wing, they were close enough. To replicate the hinges along the access panels, thin stretched sprue was glued along the hinge lines and sanded down. The fuselage was sanded down with a 4,000-grit Micro-Mesh cloth to remove any remaining high spots left over from scribing and riveting.

All four of the exhaust outlets on the fuselage are molded solid and I wanted to open them for a touch of added realism. The two bottom exhaust outlets were easily done, but the way the inside of the fuselage was molded meant that there was not enough plastic around the two side exhaust outlets to work with without damaging the fuselage. So these stayed closed and black paint was used to give the illusion of an opening.

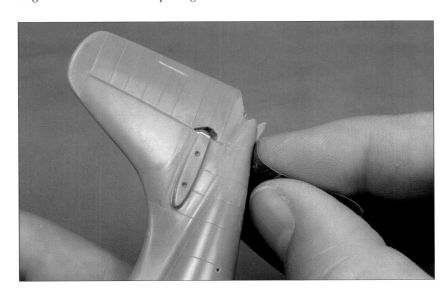

The Tamiya tail was slightly wider than the Sword piece, but by building up layers of CA glue and repeated sanding, it was blended all together.

The lower Tamiya wing is removed from the lower fuselage with a scriber.

An outline of the Tamiya wing is scribed onto clear acetate to make a locating template for the support rods.

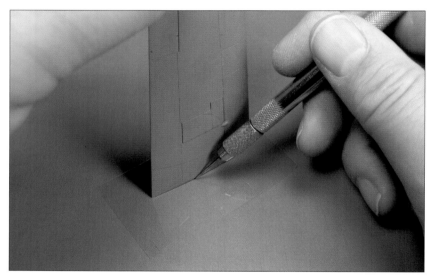

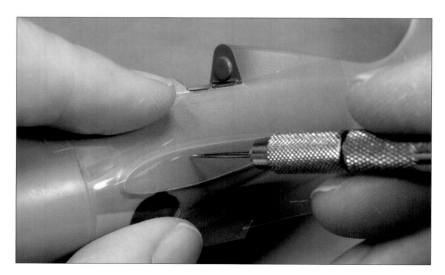

Holding the template over the wing root outline on the Sword fuselage, location marks are made for drilling.

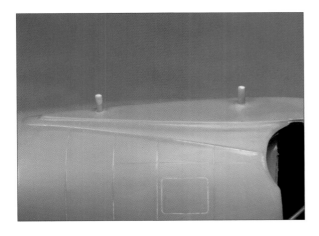

The wing support rods in place.

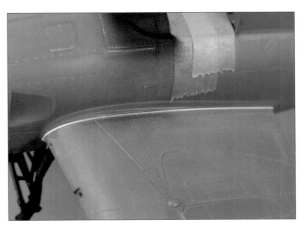

Styrene rod was glued over the wing root gap using thin liquid cement.

The wing root is sanded smooth using sandpaper wrapped around a piece of foam egg carton.

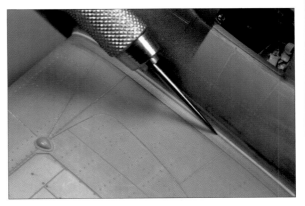

The panel lines along the wing root were rescribed using vinyl tape and a compass point.

The wings and engine have been installed and it's almost time to paint. Note the support rods for the horizontal stabilizers.

Improving the engine

As luck would have it, I had stumbled across a KMC Resin Wright 1820-56 engine at a model show. Unfortunately, KMC is no longer in production and the engine is difficult to find. The kit's engine mounts onto a raised portion of the engine bulkhead. Since the KMC resin engine was going to be used, the raised area on the bulkhead had to be sanded down to get the proper clearance for the engine in relation to the cowl opening.

The engine bulkhead was then glued in place using five-minute epoxy cement. The KMC engine piece that intrudes into the wheel well was glued onto the back of the bulkhead. This also served to hide the rather large hole in the middle of the kit bulkhead.

I painted the engine crankcase with Gunze Sangyo H337 Grayish Blue. Mixing in a little Gunze Sangyo H401 Dark Grey was used for shading. The engine cylinders were done in Tamiya XF-16 Flat Silver and the pushrods were painted Tamiya X-18 Semi-Gloss Black.

The engine was then given a pin wash with a mix of charcoal gray and burnt umber oils, mixed with enamel thinner. Several light washes were applied until the desired effect was achieved.

A placard from the Archer Fine Transfers German Information Placards set was used for the data plate at the bottom of the engine. It had the perfect look and, fortunately, it's too small to read.

Reworking the tail

The rudder on the Sword kit does not have the opening through which the elevator control rod passes. I cut an opening through the rudder, using the Tamiya rudder as a template to mark out the space to be removed. The Tamiya rudder was placed up against the kit's rudder and the shape of the opening scribed onto the rudder.

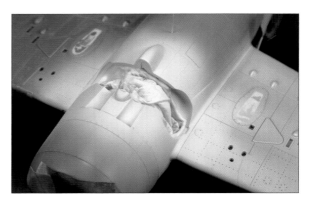

ABOVE The wheel well was well masked to avoid any overspray getting into the compartment.

ABOVE A pin wash was applied to the panel lines to provide some contrast with the paint color.

BELOW The Atlantic paint scheme consisted of dark gull gray over white. The demarcation lines between the colors were masked with rolls of silly putty.

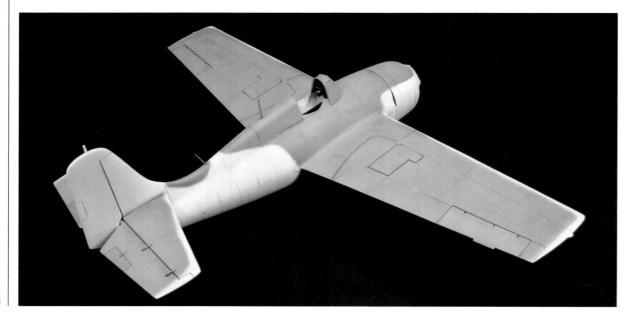

Holes were then drilled into the scribed area and the space opened up using a No. 11 hobby knife blade and a file until the proper shape was attained.

The tail end of the fuselage on the Sword kit was sorely lacking in any detail (no light, arresting hook or tow bar). At first I considered scratch-building this area, but as the Tamiya kit already had all the necessary detail, why not use it? The tail cone from the Tamiya kit was cut away with a saw and grafted onto the Sword fuselage. Using CA glue and sandpaper, it was blended into the Sword fuselage and fit perfectly. The wire antenna post atop the rudder was borrowed from the Tamiya kit and glued in place.

Giving it wings

I had originally intended to use the kit wings, but when I realized they lacked so much detail I decided to try to graft the Tamiya Wildcat wings to the kit fuselage. The Tamiya wings would still need to be modified by removing the outer wing guns and the underwing oil coolers.

Since the Tamiya lower wings and lower fuselage are one piece, the wings had to be cut away. The bottom half of the Tamiya wing was removed from the lower fuselage section by repeated scribing with a Hasegawa scriber. The cuts were made along the wing root panel line until the wing came free. As the cuts were made, the wing was carefully bent open to avoid creating a "V"-shaped grove with the scriber.

The oil coolers on the bottom of the Tamiya wing had to be removed to model the FM-2, as only the oil-cooler panel outline can be seen. The raised center of the oil-cooler base was cut off, and the remaining gaps filled in with Apoxie Sculpt putty. Once this had dried, it was sanded smooth to replicate the panel fairing left over by the removal of the oil cooler.

There were no locating tabs for the Sword kit's wings and, having cut the wings off the Tamiya kit I couldn't expect to find any locating tabs on those wings either. So a template was made for the wings for the purpose of aligning two .05in. styrene rod pins to help with reinforcing the wings. A piece of clear acetate was cut out and laid on the worktable. One of the now-assembled Tamiya wings was laid on top of the clear acetate. Using a compass point, the outline of the wing root was scribed onto the acetate. As the outline of the Tamiya wing and the outline of the wing-root area on the Sword fuselage were almost identical, the scribed airfoil shape could be laid over the fuselage wing outline and two points

The Tamiya wings and landing gear blend well with the Sword fuselage. Note the new tail and the absence of the underwing oil coolers.

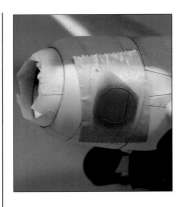

The Squadron insignia that came with the Techmod decal sheet did not have a colored background, so this was painted Gunze Sangyo H42 Blue-Gray.

marked out with the compass point for drilling. These had to be carefully chosen to avoid drilling into the wheel well or cockpit. The advantage of using the clear acetate is that the same template can be used for both sides of the fuselage. Once all of the positions were marked off, holes could be drilled for the placement of styrene reinforcing pins.

To attach the wings, the landing gear was first set in place for the fuselage to rest on. The fuselage was then measured on each side to ensure that it was level on the gear. The wings were attached, making sure the correct dihedral was achieved. Epoxy glue was again used for its extra strength and working time when compared to CA glue. Once both wings were attached, a measurement was taken at the wing tips to make sure they had the same dihedral. They were left to dry, with the measurements checked every few minutes. The stabilizers were then attached in the same manner.

The unnatural act of mating the fuselage and wings from two different kits not unexpectedly left a noticeable gap along the wing roots. Styrene rod was glued along the gaps using Tamiya thin cement, working the rod into the opening as the styrene began to soften. Once dry, the high areas of the rod were taken down with a Dremel tool and a small grinding bit. The seam was then sanded down using sandpaper wrapped around a piece of foam egg carton. Any remaining small gaps were filled in with CA glue and sanded smooth. No external wing tanks are included with the Sword kit, so the tanks from the Tamiya kit were used. To better replicate the flexible fuel hose attaching the tank to the wing, .04in. insulated black wire was used. This fit perfectly into the hole on the bottom side of the wing. Removing the insulation and drilling a .02in. hole into the tank allowed the wire to fit perfectly into the tank receptacle.

Painting

I started by spraying the undersides with a white mix of five parts Gunze Sangyo H11 Flat White and one part Gunze Sangyo H338 Light Gray. The gray was added to the mix to take the edge off the white. Silly putty and wet paper towels were used to mask around the opening of the wheel well. Gunze Sangyo H317 Gray was used for the upper surface dark gull gray color, using rolled silly putty to mask the demarcation line between the two colors. The fabric-covered control surfaces on the upper wing were lightened with a touch of light gray paint added to the dark gull gray.

The upper surfaces of a Wildcat in the Atlantic wouldn't weather and fade like the Wildcats in the Pacific, so I wanted the weathering to be more subtle but still show some contrast in the paint. The gray color was randomly lightened in areas by the addition of some white to the base color. Then adding a dark grey to the base color created some shading.

Gunze Sangyo H21 Off-White was used for the white-colored control surfaces to add some contrast to the white paint. This was also randomly sprayed on the lower surfaces.

A tape mask was cut out and used as a guide when painting the upper gray for the fuselage sides, so I would know where to spray the gray paint demarcation line in relation to the national insignia.

The engraved lines around the control surfaces and access panels were pinwashed with charcoal gray oil paint. The panel lines were washed with a dark gray oil mix to provide some contrast with the upper surface color. I wiped off the excess wash with a cotton swab dampened with Turpenoid. Once the painting was complete, the upper surfaces were sprayed with Pollyscale Flat finish. As the lower surfaces had a gloss finish, Pollyscale Satin was used as the final coat on these surfaces. Gray and white pigments were used on the upper control surfaces to give them more definition and add a touch of weathering.

Black Smut and Light Earth CMK Stardust pigments were used to make the exhaust stains, and the tires were given a brushing of MMP Light Air Gray pigment. Lastly, I added some paint chipping with a dark silver artist's pencil.

ABOVE The wire antenna was made from smoke-colored invisible thread. The two antennas located on the top and bottom of the fuselage were made from stretched sprue.

BELOW The gray over white paint scheme was considered more effective in the cloudy Atlantic skies than the standard Navy scheme.

ABOVE The grafted Tamiya tail can be seen to good effect here. The Tamiya wings also worked well with the Sword fuselage.

BELOW The tape over the gunports was made from Bare Metal foil. Small squares were cut out using a metal template and a hobby knife. The squares were then painted with Gunze Sangyo H21 Off-White to contrast with the white on the leading edge of the wing.

A cat takes to water – converting the Tamiya F4F-4 to the F4F-3S Wildcatfish

Subject:	Grumman F4F-3S
Kit used:	Tamiya F4F-4 Wildcat (61304)
Skill level:	Master
Scale:	1/48
Additional detailing sets used:	RVHP Wildcatfish conversion set (4801); Eduard Wildcat photo-etch set (EDU49246); Part F4F Wildcat photo-etch set (S48-027); Aires F4F detail set (4058); Cutting Edge N-3 gunsight (CEC48174); Squadron F4F canopy (9556); Tamiya M1A1 Abrams (35269); Tamiya Swordfish (61079); Tamiya Me-109E (61063); Tamiya Mosquito (61062)
Markings:	Painted, using Montex F4F mask set (48030)

The two main points of interest in this build were the scratch-built radio compartment and the floats. The radio compartment was pretty much going to be a labor of love, as little of it was going to be visible once the model was together. The floats would be from the RVHP resin float set that contains parts for the floats, beaching gear, auxiliary ventral fins and a plug for the wheel well opening. The

The Wildcatfish. Certainly an attention-getting aircraft, if there ever was one.

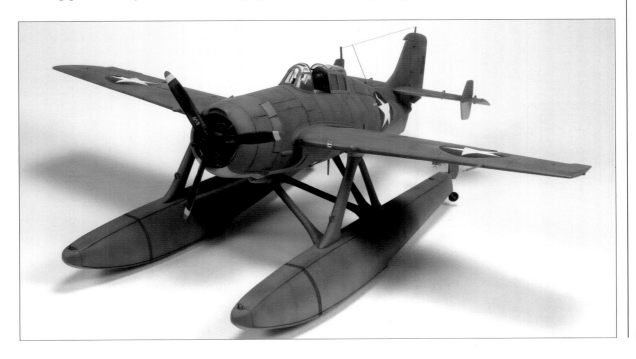

The RVHP resin float set is currently the only option available if you wish to build an F4F-3S.

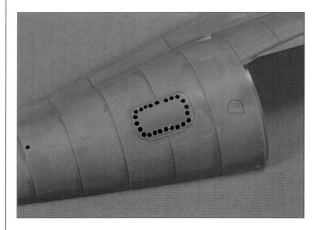

Construction starts by first removing the radio compartment door. All of the raised rivets on the fuselage and wings were removed.

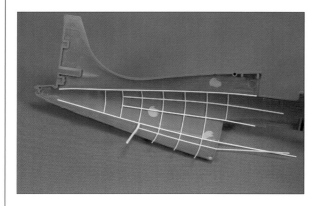

The interior framework is made from styrene strip. Several ejection-pin marks had to be filled that may have otherwise been visible.

resin parts in my set had a rough finish and the floats and struts were riddled with air holes. There are no indicators on the floats for positioning of the struts and the instructions consist of little more than three drawings.

Fuselage radio compartment

The first order of business was to remove the radio compartment door by first drilling holes around the perimeter and then using a hobby knife to connect the dots. A file and sandpaper were then used to clean-up and shape the opening.

Before any interior components could be installed, the interior framework had to be laid down, which consisted of styrene strips laid out to correspond to the rivets on the outside of the fuselage. Once this foundation was complete, the interior was sprayed with Gunze Sangyo H325 Gray, which is a good match for the Grumman Gray used by Grumman Aircraft on much of the fuselage interior spaces.

Building the various components for the interior was simply a matter of cutting, shaping and gluing various pieces of styrene together until you got the shape you wanted. The Aero Detail book on the Wildcat has a detailed illustration in ¼ scale that shows the interior details, which was quite useful for sizing and placing the various components.

Raiding the spare parts box is often easier and quicker than trying to fabricate your own parts. The flap control vacuum tank located on the rear bulkhead was made from a piece that came from a Tamiya Abrams tank kit. To make its rounded ends, Apoxie Sculpt putty was applied and, once dry, sanded to the proper shape. The auxiliary fuel tank located beneath the vacuum tank was made from a Tamiya Swordfish fuel tank. The tank was cut down to the proper size and the straps made from .01in. styrene strip.

The electrical cabling in the compartment came from .15in. and .22in. solder wire and the control cables were .006in. stainless steel wire.

Cockpit

For the construction of this cockpit, I thought I would pick the best parts from different cockpit sets and try to mold them into a workable cockpit. The cockpit turned out to be a medley of Aires resin (floor, rear bulkhead and seat), Tamiya plastic (instrument panel, side consoles, rudder pedals), Eduard photo-etch parts and scratch-building.

Before building could really commence, the resin floor needed to be repaired. The resin edges of the cockpit foot troughs were so thin that they were mostly broken upon arrival. The remains were cut away and replaced with .01in. strip styrene. The Aires resin parts were then primed with Mr Surfacer 1000. This not only prepared the parts for painting, but helped smooth out the slightly rough surface of the resin.

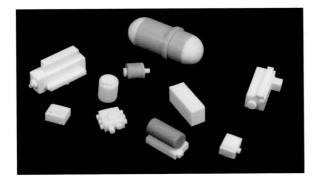

Constructing the radio compartment components was mostly just a matter of cutting and punching out basic shapes and gluing them together.

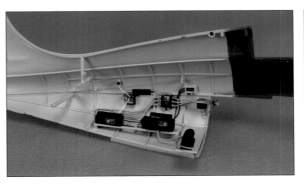

Most radio compartment components are all in place, except for a few control cables. To replicate the data plates on the electronic components, placard decals from Mike Grant Decals were used. Components were painted with Tamiya X-18 Semi-Gloss Black.

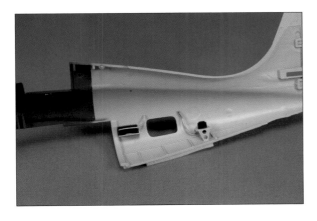

On the right side of the interior I only built detail that could be seen near the edge of the compartment door, in this case the battery and compass. The two cockpit lights were made from styrene and solder wire.

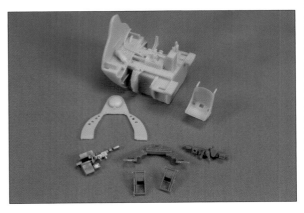

Aires resin and Tamiya kit parts made up the bulk of the cockpit. Eduard photo-etch and scratch-building would do the rest.

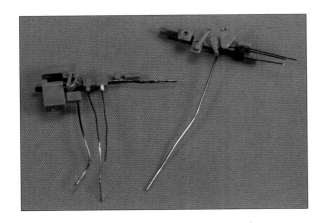

The Tamiya cockpit side consoles were detailed with various thicknesses of copper, brass and solder wire to represent cables and control linkages.

A black/brown wash was done in the corners and recesses to add shadows and depth.

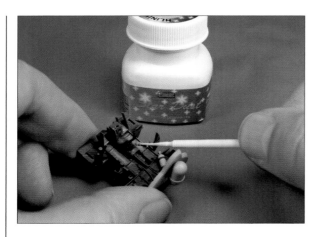

Paint wear on the foot troughs was done using CMK Stardust Aluminum pigment and a micro brush. I find that the CMK pigments work well for this type of weathering as they adhere better to the paint than the other brands of pigments.

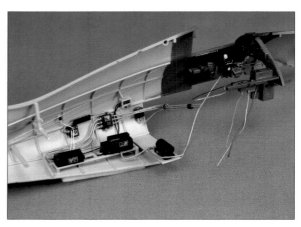

The completed instrument panel and side consoles had to be attached prior to the cockpit assembly. Then the cockpit would be inserted from underneath between the side consoles.

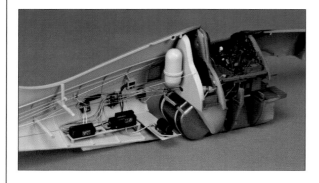

All control cables, radio compartment components and cockpit are now in place.

Strips of styrene had to be glued to the top of each end to close a sizable gap and provide a decent fit for the wheel well plug.

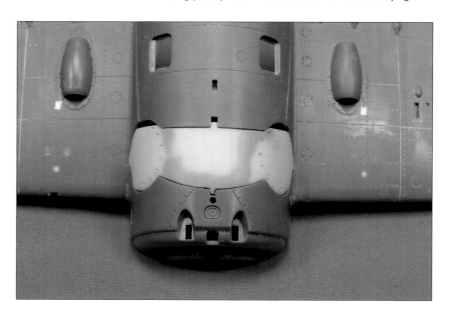

The F4F-3S had its landing gear removed and the opening faired over. It took a fair amount of sanding and filing to get the resin insert to fit properly.

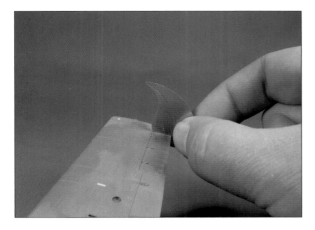

To remove the ailerons, first the edges were cut with a micro saw.

Then the front of the aileron was removed using a scribing tool.

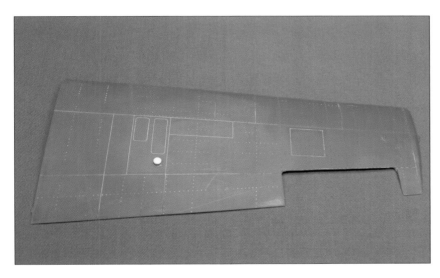

LEFT The upper wing with the removed aileron and the panel lines rescribed.

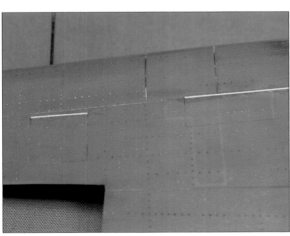

The hinges for the machine-gun ammo and flotation bags access doors wing made from .01in. styrene rod.

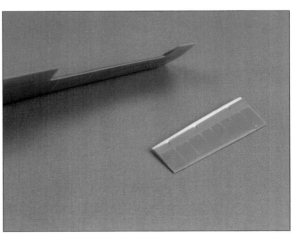

The wing space for the aileron has been reduced in thickness with a file and a strip of styrene added to the front of the aileron, sanded to the correct shape.

To remove the elevators, the extended outer tips were cut through, as this would be easier than attempting to cut around them. They would be reattached later on.

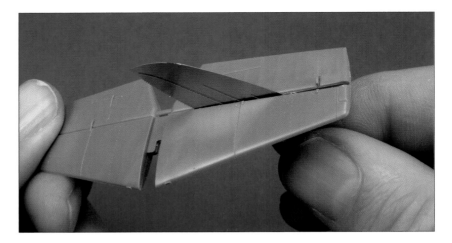

The hinge slots in the elevator were opened up with a hobby knife and sandpaper.

The modified horizontal stabilizer and elevator fit perfectly after modifications.

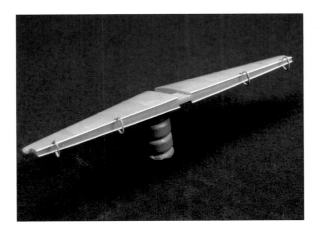

Strip styrene provided the raised edges along the rear of the horizontal stabilizer. The photo-etch hinges are from the Part set.

There is a lot going on at the tail end of the Wildcatfish. Here's a good look at the resin auxiliary stabilizers, deflected control surfaces and rebuilt tail.

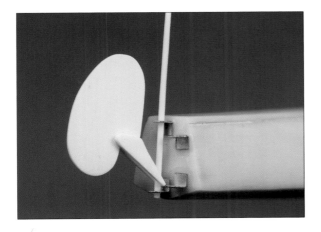

The rudders were built from styrene sheet and rod. The brackets for the rudder and tailwheels came from the spare photo-etch bin.

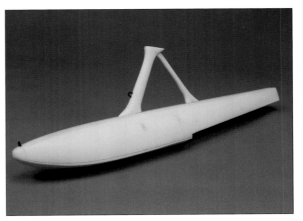

The completed main float assembly. Tie-down loops on the tip of the floats and on the front of the main strut were made from .02in. wire, bent around a drill bit.

The instrument panel hood is overly thick for the scale and was thinned down by scraping the underside with the edge of a hobby knife

Model Master Euro I Dark Green is a good match for the bronze green paint that Grumman used on their cockpits. A bit of Model Master Green Zinc Chromate was added and the mix was sprayed from above to lighten the horizontal surfaces. The cockpit details were painted with Tamiya enamels.

The cockpit components were sprayed with several coats of Future acrylic floor wax to prep them for the enamel wash. A black/brown enamel wash was done in the corners and recesses of the cockpit and a brush dampened with enamel thinner was used to remove the excess wash. This had the added benefit of adding to the weathering of the cockpit.

The control cables within the rear fuselage lead into an opening in the rear cockpit bulkhead underneath the flap control vacuum tank. In order to position the forward ends of the control cables, the cockpit assembly was going to have to be first glued onto the left fuselage half. This removed the easy option of just inserting the cockpit assembly from underneath into the completed fuselage. Using a Dremel tool, an opening was routed out of the rear bulkhead

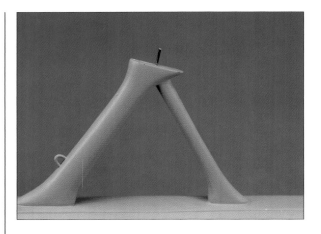

Once the floats and the main supports were completed, I attached them to the lower wing using a brass pin for extra support. Only one pin was used, as this gave enough extra strength, while allowing the strut to pivot for alignment.

A lot of filing and test-fitting went into getting the support struts properly in position. Once fitted, they were epoxied in place.

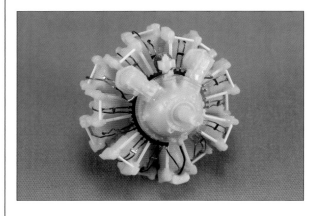

The Aires resin engine was detailed using styrene, copper wire and Eduard photo-etch parts.

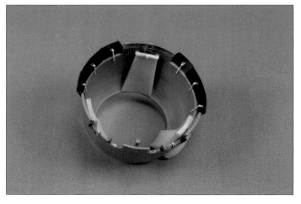

The resin air intakes and photo-etch cowl flaps added a great deal of detail and interest to the cowling.

The completed Pratt & Whitney engine looks quite convincing and, with a little fitting, sat snuggly inside the cowling.

The propeller on the Wildcatfish had the early red–yellow–blue tip markings. The yellow was painted first, being the lightest color. It was then masked off for the red, and finally the blue.

ABOVE I typically don't prime my models, but with all of the sanding, filing, drilling and general abuse the model's surface was subjected to, I decided a few coats of Mr Surfacer 1000 would help smooth everything out and reveal any areas that needed touching-up.

BELOW No need for precision here. I thought Gunze Sangyo Tire Black might be less stark as a pre-shade and blend better than straight black paint.

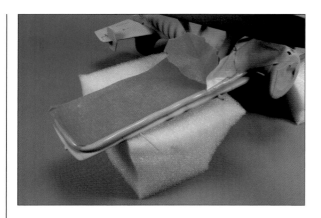

The upper blue-gray color wraps around the leading edge of the wing and was masked using silly putty.

to accept the control cables. The control cable wire could then be strung through the rear fuselage supports and attached to the opening in the rear bulkhead.

While preparing the canopy, I managed to snap it in half. Not having a spare plastic canopy, I used the Squadron vacuform canopy for the F4F that I just happened to have handy.

Fuselage

Once the fuselage halves were together, the tailwheel and tow bar were removed to make room for the resin ventral stabilizer. I attached this later by first pinning it with brass wire and then joining it with CA glue.

The resin fairing insert for the wheel well opening required a fair amount of sanding and shaping to get a good fit. Once that was in place, the kit fairing that goes between the landing gear struts on the lower fuselage was replaced by a solid resin piece.

The spare parts box again saved the day, with parts from the Tamiya Me-109E kit. Parts from the kit were used for the ventral antenna and the radio wire insulator on the outer fuselage (made from the end of a machine-gun barrel).

The tail cone had to be reshaped, as the arresting hook was removed from the F4F-3S and the opening faired over. A block of styrene was glued into the opening at the tail to fill-in the space. This was then sanded down and blended into the fuselage.

Wings

The blue-gray has been applied and the first weathering colors have been sprayed on.

The wings had to be backdated to the F4F-3 version, which had only four machine guns and non-folding wings. The machine-gun access panels and the wing-fold lines were filled in with CA glue and sanded smooth. The wing-fold blisters were removed with a chisel. On the lower wing, the holes for the drop tank supports, outer machine-gun chutes and the pitot tube were filled in with

strip styrene. Any remaining gaps were filled in with CA glue. After all of the unwanted panel lines and access panels had been removed, new panel lines and access panels for the -3 wing were rescribed. This was done using a compass point in a pin vise, with metal templates and Dymo tape as scribing guides.

The ailerons were going to be deflected, so they were removed from the wing halves using a micro saw and scriber. The ailerons were then glued together and a strip of styrene attached to the leading edge and sanded to get the correct aerodynamic shape. The openings in the wings for the ailerons were reduced in thickness for a better scale effect and to allow room to reposition the new ailerons.

Montex painting masks were used for the national insignia.

Photos of the F4F-3S wing show either a smooth leading edge or fairings over the four machine guns. In the photos showing the faired guns, the outer guns appear to have been faired over with sheet metal, while the protruding inner guns had a sheath-like fairing placed over them. As the faired guns had a more interesting look, I constructed the fairings from brass foil and the ends of rockets from a Tamiya Mosquito model.

The wing assembly was glued onto the fuselage and was a tight fit, which was not surprising considering everything that was crammed into the fuselage. The corners of the auxiliary fuel tank behind the cockpit had to be shaved down to make room for the lower wing. Slight gaps were present along the wing root and these were filled in with Mr Surfacer 500. The bottom rear of the wing assembly falls on a panel line. In order to get a clean panel line that would match the others, the space was filled in with CA glue and a new panel line was scribed on.

The elevators were removed with a micro saw so they could be repositioned in a downward deflected position. The hinge openings on the elevators were then cut open with a micro saw and the slot was opened up with the end of a No. 11 hobby blade. To smooth out the slot, sandpaper wrapped around a piece

Almost ready for an oil pin wash and some pigments to further weather the finish.

of sheet styrene of the appropriate size was worked through the slot. The leading edge of the elevator was rounded using a sanding stick. The inside of the rear edge of the horizontal stabilizer is flat, with a raised lip on either side. Rather than try to remove plastic to achieve the look, a strip of .01in. styrene was glued to the top and bottom edges to represent the raised lips. The Part photo-etch hinges for the elevator were CA glued into position and the fit was perfect.

Finally, the resin auxiliary vertical and ventral stabilizers were glued into position.

Floats

Unfortunately, there are only about half a dozen photographs available of the Wildcatfish. You will have to rely on these photos to get a good feel on how to assemble the floats' struts.

The first thing that had to be done was fill the countless number of air holes riddling the resin floats and struts. While filling and sanding the air holes, I found myself in a vicious cycle. Each time I sanded to remove the CA glue, I revealed more air holes. Before I sanded the floats down to little nubs, I filled as many as I could and called it quits, hoping that a few coats of Mr Surfacer 1000 would take care of any remaining surface irregularities.

The ends of the floats where the rudder and beaching gear's tailwheel attach are not clearly visible in any of the photographs, so the detailed construction of this area was an educated guess. The resin rudders had an odd shape to them and were pretty much useless, so they were rebuilt with styrene sheet and rod. The resin tailwheels looked undersize and definitely would not have held up to the weight of the completed model. To improve the look and beef up the gear, .032in. brass wire was used for struts, attached to two spare Tamiya Wildcat tailwheels.

Various options were weighed on how to attach the floats to the lower wing. Each alternative seemed fraught with potential problems and difficulties. I decided to attach the main float struts to the top of each float, and then attach this assembly to the lower wing. I would then proceed to fit each of the supporting struts individually.

In order to increase the working time and bonding strength, epoxy glue was used. I wish I could say I used some high-tech way to align the floats, but all I did was use the Mk I eyeball and a few measurements to check for alignment. Once the floats were attached, the model was set resting on the floats to allow them to dry. Adjustments were made until everything appeared in line. The first attempt to attach the struts with epoxy glue was a disaster. After 24 hours the glue had not set and the floats slowly peeled away from the lower wing. Either I had not mixed the epoxy in the correct proportions or I had a bad batch of glue. So I tried again with another brand of epoxy and this time everything dried solid. The supporting struts were then set in place by methodically sanding and fitting until a decent fit was found.

Prior to painting, the scratch-built float rudders were attached to their posts and angled to match the position of the rudder (they were connected to the rudder operation).

I decided not to use the beaching dolly that came with the RVHP set, as I liked the look of the plane better without it. However, the model turned out to be quite a tail-sitter, so I attached the beaching gear's tailwheels, which set the model at a much better angle. Perhaps not a correct configuration, but it at least solved the tail-heavy problem.

Engine

The kit's cowl intakes for the intercoolers were removed and the Aires resin air intakes for the intercoolers and carburettor installed. Various resin engines were considered, but the Aires resin engine was used as it had the best fit. I decided to assemble the engine prior to painting, rather than paint the parts separately and risk damaging the paint finish during assembly. The pushrods

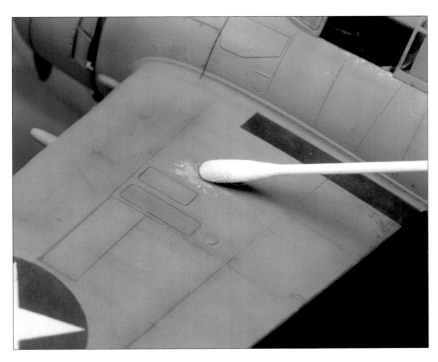

LEFT A blending stick and cotton swab were used to apply the pigments, and a little aggressive use of these added to the effect by distressing the paint.

BELOW Open cowl flaps and deflected control surfaces add interest to the model.

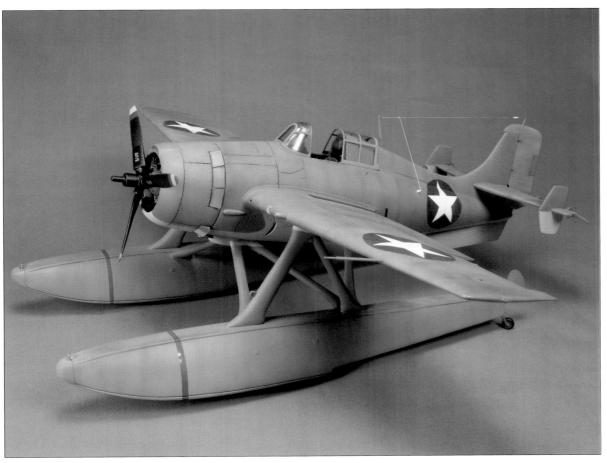

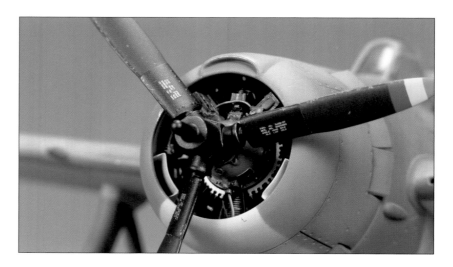

and oil transfer pipes were fabricated from different sizes of styrene rod and solder wire used to detail the engine.

After spraying the crankcase with Gunze Sangyo H42 Blue-Gray, the rest of the engine was brush painted with a combination of Tamiya enamels and Vallejo acrylics. The crankcase was given a wash of black/brown enamels and the cylinders a black acrylic wash. A very light drybrushing was then done.

The data plate on the crankcase was a German information placard from Archers Transfers. The engine was then sprayed with a 3:1 mix of Pollyscale acrylic Flat (404103) and Satin (404106).

The engine was attached to the fuselage using epoxy glue, to assure a good bond and allow time to correctly position the engine.

Painting

After a few applications of Mr Surfacer 1000, the model was pre-shaded with Gunze Sangyo H77 Tire Black. The lower surfaces were sprayed with light gray, a mix of two parts Tamiya XF-19 Sky Gray and one part XF-2 Flat White, allowing the pre-shading to slightly show through. Areas were then randomly darkened with a 50:50 mix of the light gray and sky gray and then lightened with a 50:50 mix of light gray and white. The upper surfaces were painted blue-gray: a mix of three parts Tamiya XF-18 Medium Blue and one part XF-2 Flat White. The blue-gray color wraps around the leading edge of the wing and the demarcation line was masked-off with rolls of silly putty and tape. This same method of masking was used for the fuselage as well. Adding a bit of Gunze Sanyo H338 Light Gray to the mix and thinning it down weathered the upper surfaces. This was sprayed around wear areas and randomly on the upper surfaces. Straight Tamiya XF-18 Medium Blue was sprayed on in a similar fashion to add to the weathering effect.

Montex masks were used for painting the national insignia and the striping on the floats and fuselage was masked with Tamiya tape. As the national insignia were painted with gloss Gunze Sangyo paints, they were dulled down with Pollyscale flat (404103).

A dark gray oil wash was spread around the access panels and control surfaces. All of the panel lines were left untouched, except for some light post-shading with the airbrush.

Blue and gray pigments were used to alter the color of the finish to enhance the weathering effect. While doing the oil wash, I found that by applying straight Turpenoid to the model with a brush left a subtle staining effect that gave the appearance of dried water. No final clear coat was applied to the model, as I was happy with the finish as it was. Finally, a small amount of paint wear was added with a dark gray pencil.

LEFT The open cowl flaps actually allow you to see through the engine compartment. Note the worn paint along the trailing edge of the wings.

BELOW The Wildcatfish was not able to match the performance of the Japanese Navy's A6M2-N "Rufe" floatplane.

ABOVE **A combination of paint, oils and pastels were used to weather the paint finish. Ocean air and spray could be rough on the paint surface.**

BELOW Eduard's photo-etch bomb racks were attached to the lower wings.

Building techniques

This section is to present, in a bit more detail, some of the techniques used to build the models in this book.

Removing panels and doors

Occasionally a modeller finds that he wants or needs to remove a panel or door on an aircraft. This could be to display an interior space or to replace the kit piece. This is a simple process, but one that should be done slowly and carefully. When drilling the holes, avoid starting next to the panel line, otherwise you may find that when you begin your filing and sanding, you've now enlarged the panel beyond its original size.

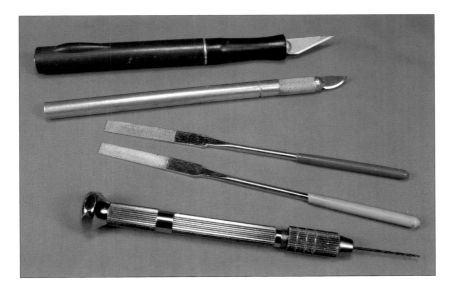

Tools for removing panels: pin vise, hobby knife and files.

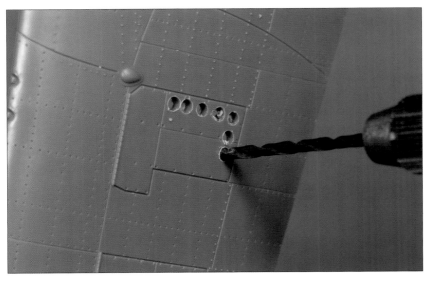

Begin by drilling holes around the perimeter of the panel you wish to remove. Avoid drilling too close to the panel line. Make the holes close enough to each other that you can easily cut through the material with a hobby knife (a couple of these holes could be closer together).

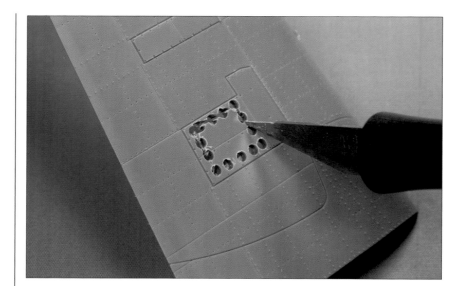

Once the holes are drilled, "connect the dots" by using a hobby knife to carefully cut through the remaining material and remove the center of the panel.

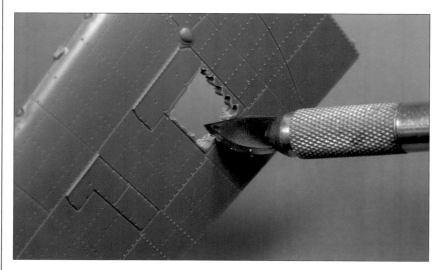

Use your hobby knife to carefully trim away the raised portions of the material and trim closer to the panel line.

Use a file to clean-up and smooth out the edges of the panel.

Filling unwanted panel lines and seams

Panel lines occasionally need to be removed on a kit for purposes of accuracy or for conversions. And despite one's best efforts, seams don't always turn out the way we would like. Cyanoacrylate (CA) glue can be used to fill unwanted panel lines and gaps in seams. This technique is also handy for filling in those inevitable slip-ups while rescribing.

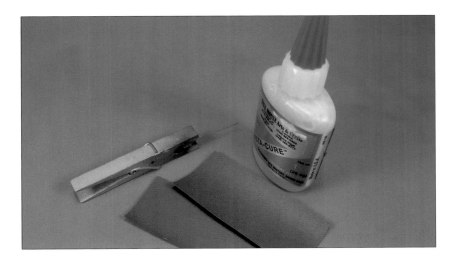

Tools for removing panel lines and filling seams: CA glue, an applicator and various grades of sandpaper.

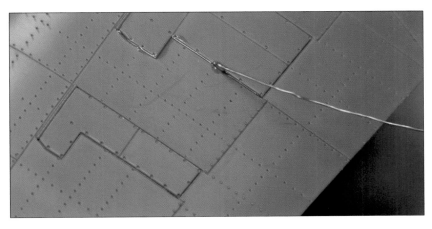

Unwanted panel lines can easily be removed by filling the groove with CA glue. Depending on the depth and width of the groove, more than one application of glue may be needed. Here, a thin wire held by a clothes pin is used as the applicator for the glue. Avoid using putty-type fillers for filling panel lines if you may be rescribing over them, as the putty will not hold up under the scriber.

Once the CA glue has dried, 400-grit sandpaper can be used to take down the ridges and smooth out the surface. Then use 600-grit sandpaper to remove any sanding marks.

Filling gaps with Mr Surfacer

Sometimes I wonder how we ever managed without this product. This can be used for filling seams (ones that won't need rescribing) and those pesky ejection-pin marks that always seem to be located in the most annoying places. Several applications may be needed, as the putty will shrink as it dries. Make sure the putty is completely dry if you decide to do any sanding.

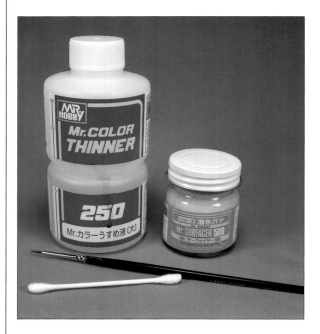

Tools for filling gaps: Mr Surfacer 500, Mr Color Thinner, a brush and a cotton swab.

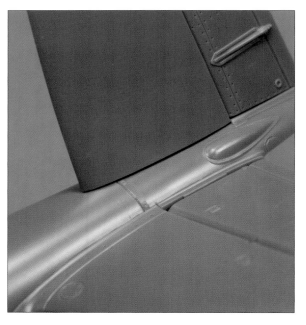

Occasionally you find yourself with a gap that needs filling, but you still want the appearance of a seam line.

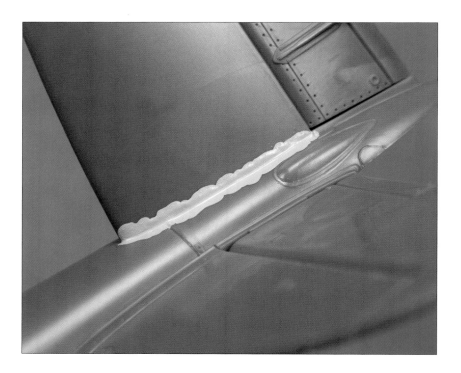

Fill the gap with Gunze Sangyo Mr Surfacer 500. Make sure it seeps down into the gap or a second application may be necessary. Allow it to dry for a few minutes.

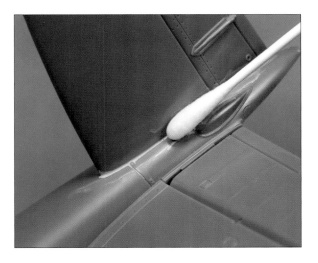

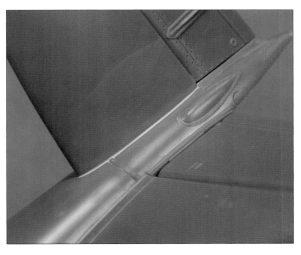

Using a cotton swab dampened with Gunze Sangyo Mr Color Thinner, gently wipe along the seam line and the excess filler will start to come off. Replace the cotton swab as it loads up with the removed filler.

You will end up with a smooth, even line that will look great under a coat of paint.

Removing scratches from clear parts

Scratching or otherwise marring the finish on clear parts is one of the most frustrating things that can happen to a modeller. A blemished canopy can ruin the appearance of an otherwise great-looking model. Fortunately, it's easy to remove scratches from clear parts. All you need are the right tools and a bit of patience. This technique can also be used to improve the appearance of clear parts right out of the box.

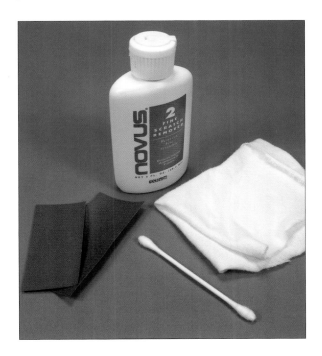

Tools used for removing scratches: Various grades of sandpaper, plastic polish, cotton swab and a buffing cloth.

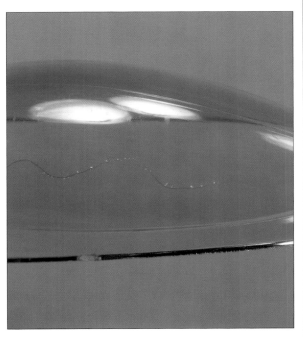

I've taken the canopy from an F-16 kit and made a deep scratch using the tip of a compass needle.

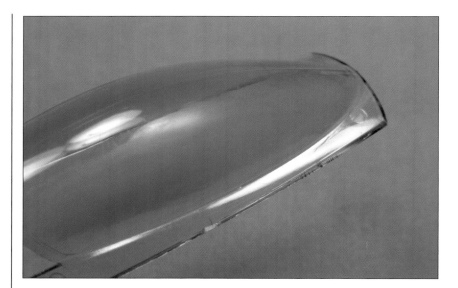

Starting with 400-grit sandpaper and working down to 1,500-grit, the area surrounding the scratch is sanded down until the scratch itself is no longer visible. Depending on the severity of the scratch, you may not need to start with a 400-grit sandpaper. The canopy now looks worse than when you started. Not to worry. Things will improve.

Using a plastic polish, such as Novus or Tamiya's brand, take a few minutes to polish out the area with a cotton swab dipped in the polish.

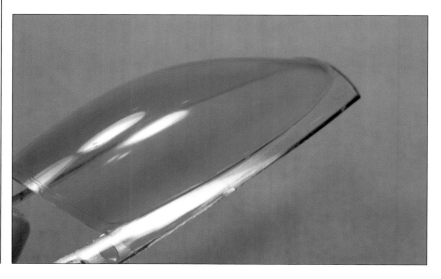

When you have finished polishing, take a soft cloth (an old T-shirt works well) and buff out the area, making sure to remove any polish residue. You will then have yourself a nice, shiny canopy that will probably look better than before it was scratched.

Rescribing

Rescribing tends to be the bane of many modelers. It is often looked upon as a technique for the "expert" modeller and therefore avoided. While admittedly, it does take a bit of practice to get the feel of it, it isn't really all that difficult. And once you have learned the technique, it opens up all sorts of new avenues to your modeling. Different scribing tools will handle and scribe differently. Learn what works for you and practice on those spare pieces of plastic.

The variety of tools used for scribing: scribers, metal templates and tapes used for scribing guides. Even with all the different scribers available, I always come back to a compass needle in a pin vise. The orange vinyl tape is a great scribing guide for curved surfaces when Dymo tape won't work.

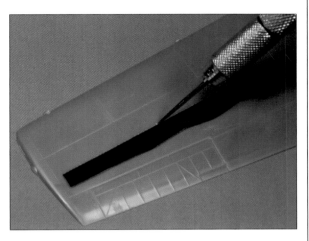

For scribing straight lines or gentle curves, Dymo label tape works well. The scriber is run along the edge were you want to scribe the line. Keep the pressure light and use multiple passes until you are happy with the line. Avoid falling into the trap of "If three strokes are good, then maybe ten will be better," or you're likely to end up with a trench.

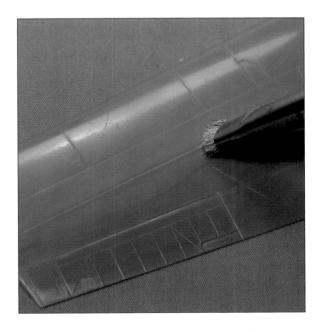

Once the line has been scribed, a few swipes with 600-grit sandpaper will knock down any raised edges. Then brush out the groove with a stiff brush.

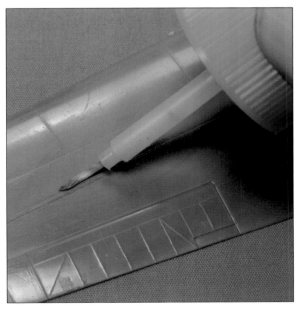

Finally, a thin line of Tamiya liquid cement will smooth out the groove and dissolve any leftover bits of plastic.

Wildcat kits and accessories

Kits available

1/144 scale	Description
Sweet	FM-2 Wildcat
Sweet	RN Wildcat VI & Flight Deck
1/72 scale	
Academy	F4F-4 Wildcat USN
Dragon	F4F-4
Eastern Express	F4F Wildcat USN
Frog Models	F4F Wildcat USN
Hasegawa	Martlet III
Hasegawa	F4F-4 Wildcat
Hobbyboss	FM-1 Wildcat
Hobbyboss	FM-2 Wildcat
Hobbyboss	F4F-3
Hobbyboss	F4F-4
Sword	FM-2

1/48 scale	
Sword	FM-2 Wildcat
Tamiya	F4F-4 Wildcat
1/32 scale	
Hobbycraft	F4F-4 Wildcat
Revell	F4F-4 Wildcat
Trumpeter	F4F-3 Wildcat
Trumpeter	F4F-4 Wildcat

1/72-scale accessories

Aires	F4F-4 resin/photo-etch cockpit
CAM Decals	F4F-3 Wildcats
CMK	F4F resin wing-fold set
CMK	F4F resin/photo-etch armament set
Eduard	F4F-4 detail (Hasegawa)
Eduard	F4F detail Zoom set (Hasegawa)
Eduard	F4F national insignia + red outline
Eduard	F4F national insignia 1941–43
Eduard	F4F canopy/wheel masks (Hasegawa)
Eduard	F4F canopy/wheel tape masks (Hasegawa)
Engine and Things	Resin P&W R-1830-76 Twin Wasp engine
Engine and Things	Resin P&W R-1830-86 Twin Wasp engine
Euro Decals	Interesting FAA Wildcats/Martlets
Mini Print Decals	F4F-4
Montex	F4F mini mask (Hasegawa)
Quickboost	F4F-4 correct cowling
Quickboost	F4F-4 engine
Quickboost	F4F-3 wing conversion
Pavla	F4F vacuform canopy
Squadron	F4F vacuform canopy
Super Scale Decals	F4F-3 Wildcats
Super Scale Decals	F4F-3/4 Wildcats
True Details	F4F resin wheels
True Details	F4F resin cockpit
True Details	F4F resin round back seats
Techmod Decals	F4F-4
Techmod Decals	FM-2
Techmod Decals	Wildcat Mk I

1/48-scale accessories

AM Tech Decals	F4F First Team Wildcats
Aires	F4F-4 resin/photo-etch cockpit
Aires	F4F resin wing-fold set
Aires	F4F-4 resin/photo-etch/metal detail set
Aires	F4F-4 resin/photo-etch gun bay
Airwaves	F4F-4 photo-etch
Aeromaster Decals	F4F Wildcat collection 2
Aeromaster Decals	RN Martlets and Wildcats 40–45
CAM Decals	F4F-3A VF-41/72, VMF-111
Cutting Edge	F4F canopy/wheel masks (Tamiya)
Cutting Edge	FM-2 canopy/wheel masks (Sword)
Cutting Edge	F4F resin control surfaces
Cutting Edge	FM-2 resin non-cuffed prop and spinner
Cutting Edge	F4F-3/4 resin cuffed prop and spinner
Cutting Edge Decals	F4F Wildcat I
Eagle Strike Decals	Grumman Martlets 41–44 Part I
Eduard	F4F-4 photo-etch flaps (Tamiya)
Eduard	F4F Color photo-etch Zoom (Tamiya)
Eduard	F4F-4 Color photo-etch (Tamiya)
CAM Decals	F4F-3A VF72/VMF-111
CAM Decals	F4F-4 Wildcat
Contact-Resine	F4F resin wheels

Cutting Edge Decals	F4F Wildcat I
Eduard	F4F canopy/wheel mask (Trumpeter)
Eduard	F4F photo-etch flaps (Trumpeter)
Eduard	F4F Wildcat nat. insignia + red outline
Eduard	F4F Wildcat nat. insignia 1941–43
Eduard	F4F-4 Wildcat photo-etch (Revell)
Eduard	F4F-4 Wildcat photo-etch (Trumpeter)
Eduard	F4F-4 big Ed set
Eagle Strike Decals	Wildcats at war
Engine and Things	Resin P&W R-1830-76 Twin Wasp engine
Engine and Things	Resin P&W R-1830-86 Twin Wasp engine
Engine And Things	Resin oil and ADI tank
E-Z Mask	F4F canopy mask (Trumpeter)
E-Z Mask	F4F canopy mask (Revell)
Grand Phoenix	F4F resin/photo-etch cockpit (Trumpeter)
J Rutman Products	F4F-4 resin wheels (Trumpeter)
Montex	F4F-4 mini mask (Trumpeter)
Montex	F4F-4 maxi mask (Trumpeter)
Techmond Decals	F4F-4 Wildcat
Verlinden	F4F-4 resin/photo-etch cockpit and guns
Wingz	F4F aces mask
Yellow Wings	Pre-WWII national markings

1/32-scale accessories

Eduard	F4F vinyl canopy/wheel masks (Tamiya)
Eduard	F4F tape canopy/wheel masks (Tamiya)
Eduard	F4F Wildcat nat. insignia + red outline
Eduard	F4F Wildcat nat. insignia 1941–43
Engines and Things	Resin P&W R-1839-76 Twin Wasp engine
Engines and Things	Resin P&W R-1839-86 Twin Wasp engine
Euro Decals	Interesting FAA Wildcats/Martlets
E-Z Mask	F4F canopy mask
Just Plane Stuff	F4F-3/3A resin conversion for the Tamiya F4F-4
Montex	F4F maxi mask (Tamiya)
Montex	F4F mini mask (Tamiya)
Moskit	F4F metal exhausts
Part	F4F-4 photo-etch detail
Quickboost	F4F-4 engine (Tamiya)
Squadron	F4F vacuum form canopy set
Super Scale Decals	F4F-3 Wildcats
Super Scale Decals	F4F-3/4 Wildcats
Tally Ho Decals	Wildcat national insignia mask
Techmond Decals	Wildcat Mk VI
Techmond Decals	FM-2 Wildcat
Teknics	F4F resin/photo-etch cockpit
True Details	F4F resin wheels
True Details	F4F resin cockpit
Ultracast	F4F resin seats
Ultracast	F4F resin early style seats
Verlinden	F4F-4 resin/photo-etch update set
Verlinden	F4F-4 resin/photo-etch cockpit/guns
Wingz	F4F-4 aces mask
Yellow Wings	USA national markings 1919–42 part I

Museums and collections

Most of the Wildcats still in existence today are in the form of static displays. There are a few FM-2s that have been restored to flying condition.

Grumman F4F-3	National Museum of Naval Aviation, NAS Pensacola, Florida
Grumman F4F-3	O'Hare International Airport, Chicago, Illinois
Grumman F4F-3	Cradle of Aviation Museum, Garden City, New York
Grumman F4F-3A	National Museum of Naval Aviation, NAS Pensacola, Florida
Grumman F4F-4	San Diego Air & Space Museum, San Diego, California
Eastern Aircraft FM-1	Valiant Air Command, Titusville, Florida
Eastern Aircraft FM-1	National Air and Space Museum, Washington, DC
Eastern Aircraft FM-2	Palm Springs Air Museum, Palm Springs, California (flying)
Eastern Aircraft FM-2	National Museum of the Pacific War, Fredericksburg, Texas
Eastern Aircraft FM-2	Plans of Fame, Chino, California (flying)
Eastern Aircraft FM-2	National Museum of Naval Aviation, NAS Pensacola, Florida
Eastern Aircraft FM-2	Yanks Air Museum, Chino, California (flying)
Eastern Aircraft FM-2	Museum of Flight, Everett, Washington
Eastern Aircraft FM-2	Marine Corps Air Station, Miramar, California
Eastern Aircraft FM-2	Cavanaugh Flight Museum, Addison, Texas (flying)

Further reading, video and websites

Books

Nohara, Shigeru, Aero Detail 22: *Grumman F4F Wildcat*, Dai Nippon Kaiga: Tokyo, 1998

Yuzawa, Yutaka, *Famous Airplanes of the World: Grumman F4F Wildcat*, Bunrindo: Tokyo, 1998

Cornier, Zeke, Schirra, Wally, and Woods, Phil, *Wildcats to Tomcats, The Tailhook Navy*, Phalanx Publishing: St Paul, MN, 1997

Dann, Richard, *F4F Wildcat in Action*, Squadron/Signal Publications: Carrollton, TX, 2004

Dann, Richard, *Walk Around 4: F4F Wildcat*, Squadron/Signal Publications: Carrollton, TX, 1995

Doll, Thomas, *Marine Fighting Squadron One-Twenty-One (VMF-121)*, Squadron/Signal Publications: Carrollton, TX, 1996

Greene, Frank, *The Grumman F4F-3 Wildcat*, Profile Publications: Windsor, 1971

Kinzey, Bert, *F4F Wildcat in Detail*, Squadron/Signal Publications, Carrollton, TX, 2000

Kohn, Leo, *Pilot's Handbook for Grumman Wildcat*, Aviation Publications: Appleton, WI, 1978

Lambert, John, *Atlantic Air War: Sub Hunters vs. U-Boats*, Specialty Press: North Branch, MN, 2000

Lambert, John, *Wildcats Over Casablanca*, Phalanx Publishing: 1992

Mackay, Ron, *Fleet Air Arm, British Carrier Aviation, 1939–1945*, Squadron/Signal Publications: Carrollton, TX, 2001

O'Leary, Michael, *Grumman CATS*, Osprey Publishing Ltd: London, 1992

Styling, Mark and Tillman, Barrett, *Blue Devils*, Osprey Publishing, Ltd: Oxford, 2003

Tillman, Barret, *The Sundowners*, Phalanx Publishing: St. Paul, MN, 1992

Tillman, Barrett, Aircraft of the Aces 3: *Wildcat Aces of World War 2*, Osprey Publishing Ltd: London, 1995

Tillman, Barrett, *Wildcat: The F4F in World War II*, Naval Institute Press: Annapolis, MD, 2001

Treadwell, Terry, *Ironworks*, Tempus: Stroud, 2000

Zbiegniewski, Andre, and Janowicz, Krzysztof, *Grumman F4F Wildcat*, Kagero: Warsaw, 2004

Video

F4F Wildcat DVD. (Aircraft Film) www.aircraftfilms.com/index.htm

Websites

Naval Historical Center:
http://www.history.navy.mil/photos/ac-usn22/f-types/f4f.htm
Grumman F4F Wildcat:
http://users.skynet.be/Emmanuel.Gustin/history/f4f.html
Grumman Wildcat in FAA Service:
http://www.clubhyper.com/reference/wildcatfaaba_1.htm
Fleet Air Arm Archive:
http://www.fleetairarmarchive.net/Aircraft/MartletWildcat.htm
U.S. Warplanes:
http://www.uswarplanes.net/wildcat.html

Index

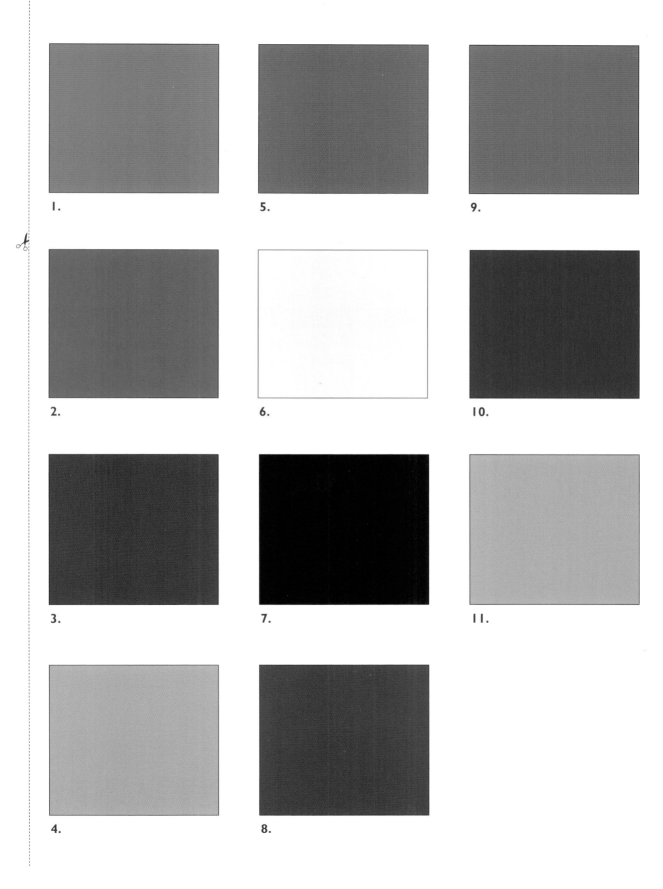

1.

5.

9.

2.

6.

10.

3.

7.

11.

4.

8.

9. Interior green

Cockpit color for late F4F-4s. Standard color for all interior surfaces, including cockpit and upper landing gear struts on General Motors-produced FM-1s and Fm-2s. Similar to FS 24151.

5. Dark gull gray

Topside of aircraft operating over the Atlantic. Similar to FS 36231.

1. Middle stone

Used as an upper surface camouflage color by the RAF and Royal Navy in North Africa. Similar to FS 30266.

10. Bronze green

Cockpit color for F4F-3s and early F4F-4s. Similar to FS 24052.

6. Insignia white

Lower color of US Navy aircraft beginning January 1943, and aircraft operating over the Atlantic. Used as part of the tri-color paint scheme. On Atlantic-based aircraft, gloss white would be used on the undersides, transitioning to a non-specular white on horizontal surfaces. Similar to FS 37880.

2. Azure Blue

Found on the lower surfaces of RAF and Royal Navy aircraft used in North Africa. Similar to FS 35231.

11. Grumman Gray

Grumman-built Wildcats had a unique primer for the fuselage interior spaces, other than the cockpit. This took the place of the place of zinc chromate/interior green and is commonly referred to as Grumman Gray. It is very similar to light gray, FS 36440.

7. Sea blue

After 1942, the top wing surfaces of US Navy aircraft were painted semi-gloss sea blue. The top fuselage surfaces were painted in non-specular sea blue. Used as part of the tri-color paint scheme. Similar to FS 25042/35042.

3. Blue gray

Topside color for US Navy aircraft until 1942. Phasing-in began in August 1941, as a change from all light gray-colored aircraft. Similar to FS 35189.

8. Intermediate blue

Fuselage sides of US Navy aircraft after 1942. Used as part of the tri-color paint scheme. Similar to FS 35164.

4. Light gray

Lower surfaces of US Navy aircraft until 1942. Similar to FS 36440.